Dear Harriet,
Good luck with
new beginnings,
with best wishes,
Leora Batnitzky

Harriet...
Many Blessed Years
Al Raboteau

Princeton will not be the
same without you. You
have been a good friend
Joe Williamson

Few have done more for students,
and no one cares more about them.
For this above all, you will be
missed.
Jeff Stout

HSS—
nine-to-five would have been
radically different for me, 1991–99,
if you hadn't been here. It has
been real spice to work with you, and
I trust our camaraderie will continue
well, outside of 1879 Hall! Love, Anita

Dear Harriet,
We'll miss you — you know we'll
never be able to replace you.
Have a wonderful time.
Martha
Himmelfarb

Dear Harriet —
Thanks so much,
invaluable help over the years.
All best wishes for your
good health and happiness
in your new life.
Jackie Stone

Dear Harriet
We love you!
Elaine Pagels

Harriet —
You've made 1879 Hall a wonderful
place to work. We'll miss you —
and envy your fresh start in
life. With love,
Buzzy
Teiser

Harriet,
Best Wishes on your
retirement... enjoy!
Patty B.

Dear Harriet —
Thanks so much for
your kind work orienting
me to the department
this year. Will miss your
wry sense of humor —
and your assistance with
all machines!
(Griffith) Warmest wishes,
Marie

Princeton University *The First 250 Years*

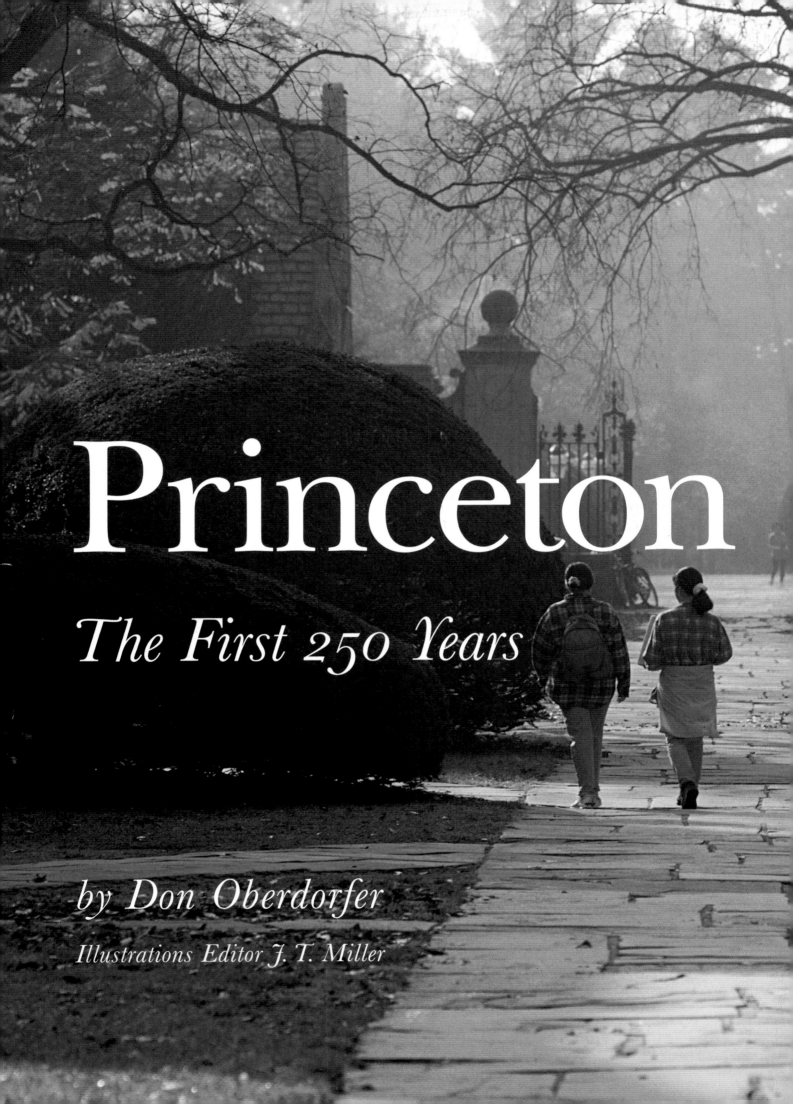

Princeton

The First 250 Years

by Don Oberdorfer

Illustrations Editor J. T. Miller

University

Published under the auspices of the Steering Committee for Princeton's
250th Anniversary,
Burton G. Malkiel *64, *Chair*
Dorothy L. Bedford '78, *Executive Director*

With the assistance of
The Office of Communications and Publications,
Justin Harmon '78, *Director*
Mahlon Lovett, *Associate Director for Publications*
Sally Freedman, *Associate Director for Communications*

The University Archives, Seeley G. Mudd Manuscript Library,
Ben Primer, *Archivist*
Nanci Young, *Assistant Archivist*

Acknowledgements and credits begin on page 270.

Executive Editor: Robert K. Durkee '69
Designer: Phillip Unetic
Assistant Designer: Lori Cohen
Printed in Italy by Mondadori

Library of Congress Cataloging-in-Publication Data
Oberdorfer, Don.
    Princeton University: The First 250 Years /
    Don Oberdorfer: Illustrations Editor, J. T. Miller.
        p. cm.
    ISBN 0-691-01122-2 (cl: alk. paper)
    1. Princeton University—History. I. Title.
LD4608.034 1995
378.749'65—dc20   95-20342

Hardcover International Standard Book Number: 0-691-01122-2

*Opening page: Triangle per-
former Wallace H. Smith '24
in the 1922-23 production,*
The Man from Earth.
*One of the finest comedians
in the club's history, Smith
later wrote the lyrics and
music for one of Triangle's
most famous songs, "Ships
that Pass in the Night."*

*Title page: View looking
south through Henry-'01
Courtyard, 1995.*

Contents

Foreword

Princeton University's first 250 years have been filled with trials and challenges as well as accomplishments, great and small. It is a colorful history, from the college's beginnings in 1746 in a parsonage in Elizabeth, New Jersey, and its move a decade later to Nassau Hall, to its development into one of the world's great institutions of teaching and learning.

Along the way Princeton has played a leading role in creating a new nation; in shaping American higher education through the academic initiatives of James McCosh, Woodrow Wilson and other forceful personalities; in preparing undergraduates and graduate students for positions of leadership in all fields of endeavor; in expanding and transmitting knowledge through faculty who are both scholars and teachers of the first rank; in introducing intercollegiate athletics; and in many other areas.

In preparing remarks for my inaugural as Princeton's 18th president I found it helpful to "converse" with each of my 17 predecessors—directly or through their writings—in an attempt to understand the goals they pursued, the choices they made and the ways in which they responded to the circumstances of their times. Now as we celebrate Princeton's 250th anniversary and prepare for a new millenium, it seems to me fitting that we should reflect more broadly on how Princeton came to be what it is today.

To tell the story, we turned to Don Oberdorfer '52, a distinguished journalist for 25 years on the *Washington Post* and an occasional visiting professor on our campus. We asked him to immerse himself in Princeton's history and then report what he found—warts and all. Don has succeeded beyond even our greatest hopes in painting a living portrait of Princeton that is honest and warm, familiar and new, thoroughly engaging and eminently readable.

For the parallel task of combing the archives, libraries and campus for illustrations, we enlisted J. T. Miller '70, a gifted photographer, whose persistence and resourcefulness have unearthed hundreds of extraordinary images of Princeton past and present. The result is a visual as well as verbal feast.

The book's first seven chapters focus on the pivotal moments of Princeton's first 200 years. The remaining seven sketch the major developments of the post-World War II era, including an increased diversity of the student body, an expanded commitment to graduate education and research, the decision to become coeducational and the creation of residential colleges. Interspersed are smaller sections that highlight selected aspects of Princeton. All of these words and pictures are skillfully woven into Phillip Unetic's striking design, and we hope that readers of the book will take as much pleasure from the medium as from the message.

Finally, I want to commend the Steering Committee for Princeton's 250th anniversary—and especially its chair, Professor Burton Malkiel *64, and its director, Dorothy Bedford '78—under whose auspices the book was produced. The overall editor was Robert Durkee '69, a member of the committee and the university's vice president for public affairs.

President Harold T. Shapiro

1

The Founding

One of two original volumes (previous page) that survive to the present day from the 474-volume personal book collection that New Jersey Governor Jonathan Belcher presented to Princeton in 1755, two years before his death. The two surviving books are in Firestone Library's rare books collection.

In the late 17th century, the shores of Stony Brook were inhabited by tribes of indigenous Leni-Lenape. They called the area Wapowog, and a length of their main trail became Nassau Street. Many of their artifacts have been found on campus. This woodcut is in Kort Beskrifning on Provincien Nya Swerige uti America, *by Thomas Campanius Holm, Stockholm, 1702, in Firestone's rare books collection.*

A t its start Princeton, like other early American colleges, was a child of the church. But this was a feisty offspring, born of a fierce controversy over the nature and direction of religion in an age when rawboned, headstrong America was wrestling with fundamental questions of identity. From the point of view of the established elders of the Presbyterian church, the founders of Princeton were radicals if not heretics. Expelled for their beliefs from the synod of Philadelphia, they were less bound to existing authority and more tolerant of differing views than others of their generation.

Woodrow Wilson, looking back at the beginnings from the perspective of 150 years in his famous "Princeton in the Nation's Service" address at the sesquicentennial celebration, noted that "Princeton was founded upon the very eve of the stirring changes which put the revolutionary drama on the stage—not to breed politicians, but to give young men such training as, it might be hoped, would fit them handsomely for the pulpit and for the grave duties of citizens and neighbors." Wilson observed that the founders "had no more vision of what was to come upon the country than their fellow colonists," but they knew that there were important unfilled needs for education throughout a large swath of the fast-developing colonies.

Harvard, William and Mary, and Yale, the three American colleges predating Princeton, were all strongly supported by the colonies they served, initially drawing their students predominantly from that colony alone. Princeton, however, had to find a way to survive without such official sponsorship, and do so in thinly populated New Jersey. As a result, Princeton initially drew its students from at least 12 of the 13 colonies, with hardly more than one-fourth of them from New Jersey. It was to a remarkable degree a national institution before there was a nation.

❦

The College of New Jersey, as Princeton was originally known, sprang from a split in the colonial Presbyterian church. In what historians call the Great Awakening, evangelists from England and the Netherlands preached a fiery and freewheeling style of religion, intense and personal and based more on inner experience than on the accepted doctrines of the church. The colonial adherents of this zealous movement, who were known as the New Side or New Lights, were embroiled in persistent conflict with established church leaders.

In a Philadelphia meeting in 1741 the New Lights who founded Princeton were expelled from the existing synod in a controversy over the right to ordain ministers. According to Jonathan Dickinson, a distinguished theologian and the first president of the

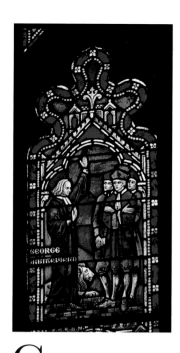

George Whitefield was a famous English evangelist whose preaching from Massachusetts to Georgia helped ignite the Great Awakening. This stained glass of Whitefield preaching from the Nassau Hall steps in 1764 is located in the University Chapel. Below: Watercolor of Dickinson parsonage in Elizabeth, from a description in an 18th-century newspaper article.

Jonathan Edwards entered Yale in 1716 when he was only 12 years old. As minister of the Northampton, Massachusetts, Congregational Church, he led the Northampton revival, which spread not only through the colonies, but to Scotland and England as well. This movement paved the way for the Great Awakening, which was particularly fostered by George Whitefield's evangelical tour in 1740. Edwards died after six weeks as Princeton's president, from a smallpox inoculation given to him by Dr. William Shippen, co-architect of Nassau Hall. Edwards' three sons all graduated from Princeton, and his daughter, Esther, was the wife of Aaron Burr, Sr., Princeton's second president. Edwards Hall (1880) was named after him. This wood statuette was carved on the back of the altar in the University Chapel by Irving and Casson in 1928.

College of New Jersey, he and three other ministers, along with three New York City Presbyterian laymen, "first concocted the plan and foundation of the college." Six of the seven founders were Yale graduates, but they considered Yale too far away and too hostile to the New Lights to claim their continuing allegiance, especially after Yale expelled a young evangelist, David Brainerd, for saying of a tutor, "I believe he has no more grace than the chair I am leaning upon." One of Princeton's founders later declared, "If it had not been for the treatment received by Mr. Brainerd at Yale College, New Jersey College never would have been erected."

At the time, no college existed between Yale in New Haven, Connecticut, and the College of William and Mary in Williamsburg, Virginia, a vast area to cover by stagecoach or on horseback. The province of New Jersey, where Dickinson and several other founders preached, seemed centrally located for the new enterprise, which was intended from the first to reach beyond the colony's borders. But the royal governor of the province, an adherent of the Church of England, refused the request for a charter for this controversial group of dissenters.

On October 22, 1746—celebrated through the subsequent centuries as the day of Princeton's founding—John Hamilton, the sick, aged and temporary successor to the uncooperative governor, granted to the seven founders a charter for the College of New Jersey "wherein Youth may be instructed in the learned Languages, and in the liberal Arts and Sciences."

There is abundant evidence that the enduring tradition of Princeton's broad role in public service and national development was born in the ideas of its very founders. "Though our great Intention was to erect a seminary for educating Ministers of the Gospel," one of the founders wrote in a letter at the time, "yet we hope it will be useful in other learned professions—Ornaments of

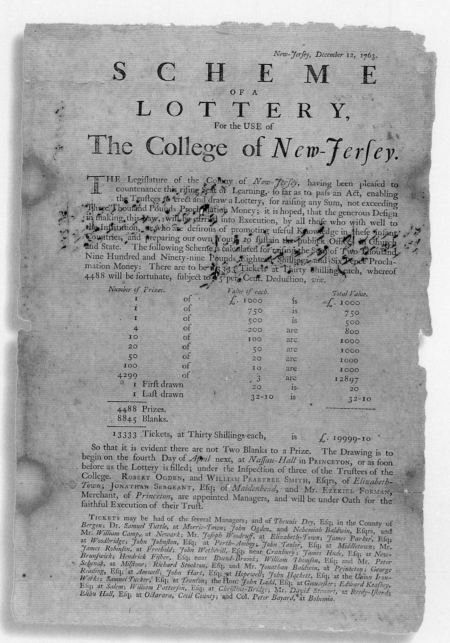

New-Jersey, December 12, 1763.

SCHEME
OF A
LOTTERY,
For the USE of
The College of New-Jersey.

THE Legislature of the Colony of New-Jersey, having been pleased to countenance this rising Seat of Learning, so far as to pass an Act, enabling the Trustees to erect and draw a Lottery, for raising any Sum, not exceeding Three Thousand Pounds Proclamation Money; it is hoped, that the generous Design in making this Law, will be carried into Execution, by all those who wish well to the Institution, or who are desirous of promoting useful Knowledge in these infant Countries, and preparing our own Youth to sustain the publick Offices in Church and State. The following Scheme is calculated for raising the Sum of Two Thousand Nine Hundred and Ninety-nine Pounds Eighteen Shillings and Six Pence Proclamation Money: There are to be 13333 Tickets at Thirty Shilling each, whereof 4488 will be fortunate, subject to 15 per Cent. Deduction, viz.

Number of Prizes.		Value of each.		Total Value.
1	of	£. 1000	is	£. 1000
1	of	750	is	750
1	of	500	is	500
4	of	200	are	800
10	of	100	are	1000
20	of	50	are	1000
50	of	20	are	1000
100	of	10	are	1000
4299	of	3	are	12897
1	First drawn	20	is	20
1	Last drawn	32-10	is	32-10

4488 Prizes.
8845 Blanks.

13333 Tickets, at Thirty Shillings each, is £. 19999-10

So that it is evident there are not Two Blanks to a Prize. The Drawing is to begin on the fourth Day of April next, at Nassau-Hall in PRINCETON, or as soon before as the Lottery is filled; under the Inspection of three of the Trustees of the College. ROBERT OGDEN, and WILLIAM PEARTREE SMITH, Esqrs, of Elizabeth-Town; JONATHAN SERGEANT, Esq; of Maidenhead, and Mr. EZEKIEL FORMAN, Merchant, of Princeton, are appointed Managers, and will be under Oath for the faithful Execution of their Trust.

TICKETS may be had of the several Managers; and of Theunis Dey, Esq; in the County of Bergen; Dr. Samuel Tuttle, at Morris-Town; John Ogden, and Nehemiah Baldwin, Esqrs, and Mr. William Camp, at Newark; Mr. Joseph Woodruff, at Elizabeth-Town; James Parker, Esq; at Woodbridge; John Johnston, Esq; at Perth-Amboy; John Taylor, Esq; at Middletown; Mr. James Robinson, at Freehold; John Wetherill, Esq; near Cranbury; James Hude, Esq; at New-Brunswick; Hendrick Fisher, Esq; near Bound-Brook; William Thomson, Esq; and Mr. Peter Schenck, at Milstone; Richard Stockton, Esq; and Mr. Jonathan Baldwin, at Princeton; George Reading, Esq; at Amwell; John Hart, Esq; at Hopewell; John Hackett, Esq; at the Union Iron-Works; Samuel Tucker, Esq; at Trenton; the Hon: John Ladd, Esq; at Gloucester; Edward Keasbey, Esq; at Salem; William Patterson, Esq; at Christine-Bridge; Mr. David Stewart, at Reedy-Island; Elihu Hall, Esq; at Octarara, Cecil County; and Col. Peter Bayard, at Bohemia.

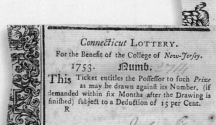

Connecticut LOTTERY.
For the Benefit of the College of New-Jersey.
1753. Numb. 2714
This Ticket entitles the Possessor to such Prize as may be drawn against its Number, (if demanded within six Months after the Drawing is finished) subject to a Deduction of 15 per Cent.
R
John Lloyd

Connecticut LOTTERY.
For the Benefit of the College of New-Jersey.
1753. Numb. 6135
Ticket entitles the Possessor to such Prize as may be drawn against its Number, (if ed within six Months after the Drawing is subject to a Deduction of 15 per Cent.
E. Bostwick

Lotteries were a common fund-raising practice in the 18th century. The trustees commissioned Benjamin Franklin to print 8,000 tickets, which were distributed in Philadelphia, New York, Boston, Virginia and elsewhere. The sketch (lower left) is from an 18th-century lottery advertisement.

Gilbert Tennent (below), son of the Reverend William Tennent who founded the Log College at Neshaminy, Pennsylvania, originally opposed the founding of Princeton, but when his father's college ceased to exist, he devoted his considerable energies to helping Princeton survive. In 1753 he sailed to Great Britain to raise funds for the new college. Tennent's portrait hangs in the Faculty Room of Nassau Hall.

The Founding

Jonathan Belcher

Jonathan Belcher was a wealthy merchant, native of Cambridge, Massachusetts, and a 1699 Harvard graduate. While Governor of Massachusetts, he promoted the cause of religious freedom. His political enemies accused him of taking bribes, and he was fired from the governorship. He went back to England to vindicate himself. Three years later, the royal court appointed him Governor of New Jersey, largely through the efforts of the New Jersey dissenters, who wanted a governor who would support their college plans. Because of his great service to the infant college, Belcher was awarded its first honorary degree, November 9, 1748, at the first commencement. The Belcher family coat of arms (below), carved in stone, stands guard above the main entrance to Firestone Library.

His Excellency. Captain General & Governor in Chief Massachuset's Bay & New Hampshire Vice Admiral — JONATHAN BELCHER Esq. of His Majesty's Provinces of NEW ENGLAND and of the Same —

As to our Embryo College it is a Noble design... I have adopted it for my Daughter which I hope may in Time become an Alma Mater to this and the Neighboring Provinces...Good Learning and a Relish for true Religion and Piety being great Strangers to this part of America.

JONATHAN BELCHER, SPRING OF 1748

the State as well as the Church. Therefore we propose to make the plan of Education as extensive as our Circumstances will permit."

Princeton's initial charter went out of its way, at the explicit demand of the founders, to guarantee the rights of conscience that were so important to them. The charter assured that "those of every religious Denomination may have free and equal Liberty and Advantages of Education in the said College, notwithstanding any different Sentiments in Religion" and declared that no student would be barred on account of his "speculative Sentiments in Religion." Richard Hofstadter and Wilson Smith, historians of American higher education, describing this as a significant change from the orthodoxies of earlier colleges, called it "a new note, imposed by the interdenominational politics of New Jersey."

Opponents of the new college disputed Governor Hamilton's authority to issue the charter, saying he had done this "so suddenly and privately" that they had no opportunity to enter objections. The fledgling college was rescued from the cloud of controversy by a new provincial governor, Jonathan Belcher, a native-born American and Harvard graduate, who issued a new and unchallengeable charter in 1748 and became a firm friend of the enterprise.

Belcher, who previously had been Governor of Massachusetts, found New Jersey a region of plenty with a good climate but deplored the absence of higher education. He wrote to one of the founders that "I am determined to adopt [the infant college] for a Child and to do everything in my power to promote and Establish so noble an Undertaking." Belcher promoted the new college wherever he could. He gave it his personal library of 474 volumes, instantly making the college library one of the largest

While attending the commencement of 1750, Belcher was seized by a severe attack of palsy. Benjamin Franklin sent him an electric machine, similar to this one, hoping it might effect some relief. Belcher's health did not improve, and remained poor for the remaining seven years of his life. This device is on display in the lobby of Jadwin Hall.

in the colonies, as well as a pair of terrestrial globes and a number of valuable personal effects. A copy of Belcher's coat of arms, which he also presented to the college, is carved along with the university's seal over the main entrance to Firestone Library.

It seems fitting, in view of its origins, that the college was first housed in a parsonage. In May 1747 the first eight or 10 undergraduates of the future Princeton University gathered for lessons at the home of Jonathan Dickinson, pastor of the First Presbyterian Church in Elizabeth, New Jersey. Dickinson had been named president the previous month by the newly formed board of trustees. The instructors were Dickinson and one of his divinity students, who served as a tutor; the dormitories, the spare rooms in the president's house or those of neighbors; the lecture hall, his parlor. Thus nearly all of the props went out from under the new college less than five months after it opened when Dickinson died suddenly of pleurisy at age 59.

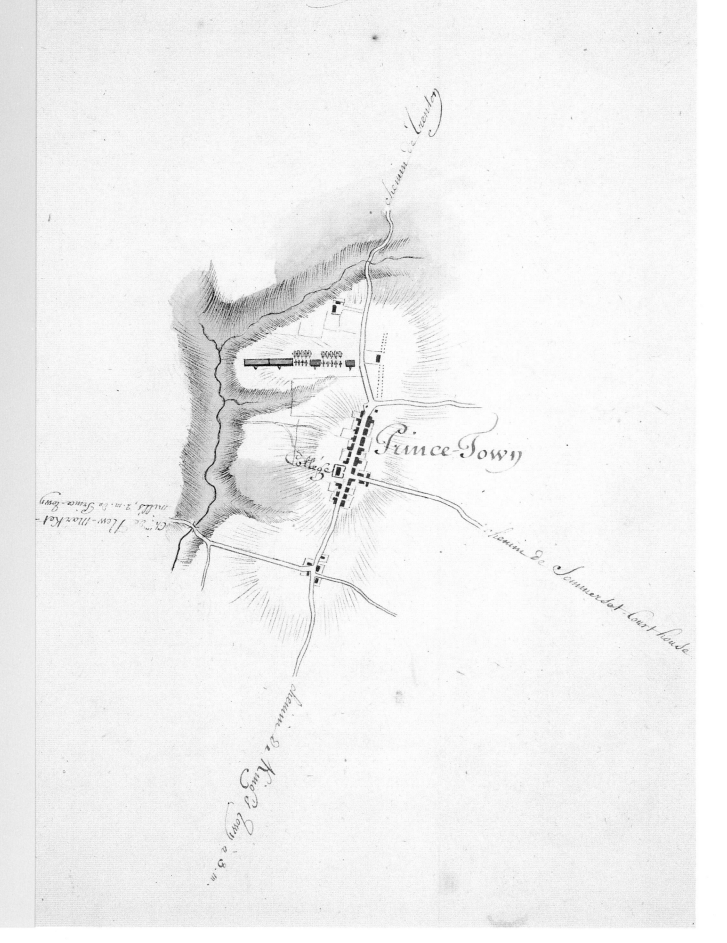

24.ᵉ Camp à **Prince-Town** le 31. Aoust, 14 miles de Sommerset Court=

Prince-Town

College

*O*riginal seal of the College of New Jersey, adopted the same day as Princeton's first commencement, November 9, 1748.

*S*cale model of an early stage coach, found recently in a New Jersey tavern. Princeton was selected as permanent site of the college over Newark, Elizabeth and New Brunswick, larger towns which also vied for it. Princeton was still a tiny village, known chiefly as a stopping place for stage coach travelers from New York to Philadelphia. It had the advantage of being far enough away from these major cities to preserve its independence, yet not so far as to be considered inaccessible.

Another of the founders was the Reverend Aaron Burr, Sr., whose name is best remembered because of his son, Aaron Burr, Jr., Class of 1772, a vice president of the United States who became infamous as the political opponent who killed Alexander Hamilton in a duel in 1804. Aaron Burr, Sr., quickly stepped into the breach left by Dickinson's death, moving the infant college to Newark, where it held its first commencement in 1748. According to Princeton's bicentennial historian, Professor Thomas Jefferson Wertenbaker, the energetic Burr was "president, professor, secretary, librarian, purchasing agent all in one." Hostile groups in the colonial legislature voted down every proposal for financial aid, leaving the college "almost without anything to support it," in the words of President Burr. In desperation, the trustees commissioned Benjamin Franklin to print 8,000 lottery tickets for the new institution. Many of the tickets were sold, but the college's ecclesiastical opponents masterminded a lawsuit that deprived the school of much of the profit.

Burr's parsonage at Newark was too close to sinful New York to suit the trustees of the struggling college. With encouragement from Governor Belcher, they launched a drive for funds and for a permanent home elsewhere in New Jersey. In January 1753 the trustees

accepted Belcher's strong recommendation that the permanent site be established at the centrally located village of Princeton. The choice of the tiny village, far from the major urban centers of the region, was a crucial one for the institution's subsequent history as a residential college, relatively insulated from distractions and society, where students lived as well as studied together. With this choice the college began to plan the imposing building that has been at its heart ever since. It would become known as Nassau Hall.

2

Nassau Hall

The First New Jersey Continental Army Regiment reenacts the final phase of the Battle of Princeton inside Nassau Hall. The January 1995 reenactment was for a film being produced for the university's 250th anniversary.

Princeton's most important building narrowly escaped being named Belcher Hall. When it was constructed in 1756, the grateful trustees of the College of New Jersey proposed to name the building for the colonial governor who had befriended and promoted their infant institution as his own child. Fortunately for generations of future Princetonians, Governor Jonathan Belcher turned down the trustees' request to "let Belcher Hall proclaim your beneficent acts" for all eternity. The governor proposed instead that the building be named Nassau Hall in memory of Britain's King William III, who was from the House of Nassau. The trustees accepted his request, averting the possibility that centuries later students and alumni would be singing passionately, "Three Cheers for Old Belcher...."

Nassau Hall, the symbol and vital center of Princeton University, celebrated in song and legend, is one of the most historic buildings in the United States. At the time of its completion it was a truly monumental structure: the largest academic building in the American colonies. Except for the nearby President's House (now Maclean House, headquarters of the Alumni Council), it was the sole building on campus until early in the 19th century. It was the place where all students roomed and ate, recited their lessons, and attended prayers and other assemblies. Later the college would branch out and grow, but Nassau Hall remained the solid foundation of its academic and residential character. It would be a central feature of the university's entire history.

Nassau Hall was occupied in the Revolutionary War by British as well as American troops, and it still shows scars from a

King William III of the House of Nassau in an engraving from a 1749 family portfolio in the iconography vault of the graphic arts collection in Firestone Library.

Coat of arms of the House of Nassau, hanging in the Nassau Club on Mercer Street.

fusillade fired against the Redcoats by a Continental Army artillery unit. The first state legislature of New Jersey met in Nassau Hall in 1776 following approval of the first state constitution. In the summer and fall of 1783 the Continental Congress met there, receiving General George Washington in public audience for the first time to render the thanks of a grateful nation, and it was there that Congress learned the British had signed a peace treaty to grant the former colonies their independence.

The thick stone walls of Nassau Hall have survived intact for centuries despite two disastrous fires and many student rebellions and protests of diverse origins. These walls have witnessed elaborate ceremonies involving many of the most eminent people of the United States—presidents, scholars, scientists, writers and artists of all sorts—as well as many renowned foreign visitors. Generations of students, faculty members, trustees, administrators and staff members have worn down the venerable building's uneven brick floor with their incessant tread on academic errands.

❧

FitzRandolph Gateway, depicted in an early 20th-century postcard, was designed by the firm of McKim, Mead and White and built with funds from descendants of Nathaniel FitzRandolph. Until 1970, when it was opened permanently, its central gate was unlocked only for special occasions.

The land on which Nassau Hall was built was contributed by Nathaniel FitzRandolph, prime mover in the small town's bid to attract the fledgling college and son of one of the original Quaker settlers of the area. FitzRandolph and several other townspeople looked on while the cornerstone of the great building was laid on September 17, 1754. The FitzRandolph Gateway, the main entrance to the campus from Nassau Street, was erected by the university in 1905 in appreciation of FitzRandolph's contribution and in fulfillment of a bequest by one of FitzRandolph's descendants. When workmen excavating for Holder Hall in 1909 came upon the remains of the FitzRandolph family burial ground, Woodrow Wilson ordered the contents of each grave placed in a separate box and reinterred under the eastern arch of Holder. A memorial tablet was placed in the arch with an English inscription by Wilson and a Latin inscription by Wilson's great academic adversary, Dean of the Graduate School Andrew Fleming West:

NEAR THIS SPOT
LIE THE REMAINS OF
NATHANIEL FITZRANDOLPH
THE GENEROUS GIVER
OF THE LAND UPON WHICH
THE ORIGINAL BUILDINGS
OF THIS UNIVERSITY
WERE ERECTED

IN AGRO JACET NOSTRO IMMO SUO

(In our ground he sleeps, nay, rather, in his own.)

According to the trustees' minutes, their original plan called for Nassau Hall to be built of brick "if good Brick can be made at Princeton & if Sand can be got reasonably cheap." The shift to stone was apparently suggested by William Worth, a Princeton mason, who stood to get the job if stone were used. Worth quarried the walls of Nassau Hall from a site on the far banks of the present Lake Carnegie. Though little known, Worth deserves to be ranked among the heroes of Princeton's history. Had brick been used instead of his mighty stone, the building might never have survived the many trials that were to come.

Students walking past the FitzRandolph memorial in the east arch of Holder Hall.

The Dawkins engraving that opens this chapter first appeared in Samuel Blair's Account of the College of New Jersey, *and apparently found its way into the 18th-century library of the New England preacher and amateur artist Jonathan Fisher. Fisher copied it using oil paints on canvas in 1807. This extraordinary primitive image of Nassau Hall was the result.*

N assau Hall's museum of geology and archaeology, circa 1879. The dinosaur skeleton in the foreground is a Hadrosaurus foulkii, found in New Jersey.

P ortrait of "Light Horse Harry" Lee, Class of 1773. He described Washington as "first in war, first in peace, and first in the hearts of his countrymen."

President Burr and the first group of students to live and work in Nassau Hall made their way on horseback in November 1756 from Newark to Princeton, where they found carpenters and plasterers still at work preparing the building. In keeping with the religious origins of the college and the spirit of the age, a two-story prayer hall in the center of the building, by far its largest room, dominated the original layout. Made even larger in the mid-19th century, it became the library, then the college museum, replete with skeletons and statuary. In 1906 it was remodeled into the current Faculty Room according to the design of Woodrow Wilson and reopened with a ceremonial speech by former U.S. President Grover Cleveland, then a Princeton resident.

Other key features of the original layout of Nassau Hall were classrooms, a kitchen, a dining area and about 40 rooms for students. Nearly all of Princeton's 18th-century students roomed here, including a future president, James Madison; a future vice president, Aaron Burr, Jr.; and "Light Horse Harry" Lee, a Revolutionary War hero and father of Robert E. Lee, commander of Confederate forces in the Civil War.

Student life in Nassau Hall was spartan. The journal of Philip Vickers Fithian, Class of 1772, recorded the following routine prior to the Revolutionary War, when there were 81 students:

5-5:30 a.m. *Dressing period.* "The Bell rings at five, after which there is an Intermission of half an hour, that everyone may have time to dress, at the end of which it rings again, and Prayers begin; And lest any should plead that he did not hear the Bell, the Servant who rings goes to every Door and beats till he wakens the Boys."

5:30 *Morning Prayers.* "After Morning Prayers, we can, now in the winter, study an hour by candle Light every Morning."

8:00 *Breakfast.* "From eight to nine is time of our own, to play, or exercise."

9:00-1:00 *Recitation.*

1:00 *Dinner.* "We dine all in the same Room, at three tables. After dinner till three we have Liberty to go out at Pleasure."

3:00-5:00 *Study.*

5:00 *Evening Prayers.*

7:00 *Supper.*

9:00 "At nine the Bell rings for Study; And a Tutor goes through College, to see that every Student is in his own Room; if he finds that any are absent, or more in any Room than belongs there, he notes them down, and the day following calls them to an Account. After nine any may go to bed, but to go before is reproachful."

The death of General Hugh Mercer was the most serious American loss in the colonists' watershed victory at Princeton. It became the dramatic central subject of John Trumbull's great historical painting in the rotunda of the Capitol in Washington, D.C. This ink wash is one of a group of six preparatory drawings for that painting which are among the iconographic treasures of Firestone Library. Nassau Hall can be seen in the distance just beyond Mercer Oak. Mercer, a doctor in civilian life, was bayoneted seven times when the British soldiers mistakenly thought he was George Washington.

Charles Willson Peale was a noted painter and a soldier in the Continental Army. He fought at the Battle of Princeton, so it was most appropriate that the college should commission him for this famous portrait (opposite) of General Washington. The portrait was completed in 1784. Behind Washington's left leg is the mortally wounded General Mercer. Mercer's son, an apprentice under Peale, posed as the model for his dying father. This painting survived both major fires in Nassau Hall.

After more than two centuries, the Mercer Oak still marks the Princeton battlefield.

Here Freedom stood, by slaughtered friend and foe,
And, ere the wrath paled or the sunset died,
Looked through the ages; then, with eyes aglow,
Laid them to wait the future side by side.

ENGLISH POET ALFRED NOYES, VISITING PROFESSOR, ON STONE PLAQUE COMMEMORATING THE BATTLE OF PRINCETON, ERECTED IN MAY 1918.

Looking back later on what he called "the most pleasant as well as the most important period" of his life, Fithian recalled with particular pleasure the foibles and escapades of life in Nassau Hall: "Meeting and Shoving in the dark entries; knocking at Doors and going off without entering; Strowing the entries in the night with greasy Feathers; freezing the Bell; Ringing it at late Hours of the Night...."

The Revolutionary War took its toll on Nassau Hall. British troops occupied the building and used it as a dormitory and a temporary jail for citizens suspected of aiding the rebels. Horses were quartered in the basement, and the library was plundered. In the Battle of Princeton in January 1777, the Continental artillery trained a withering fire on the building from where Blair Hall is today. One round hit the south wall of the building, at a spot from which the ivy on the building is carefully pruned. Another round went through the window of the prayer hall and struck a portrait of King George II.

After the war Washington agreed to the trustees' request that he sit for a portrait depicting him at the famous battle, with Nassau Hall in the background. It was placed in the frame that previously held the damaged portrait of the British monarch. The Washington portrait, by Charles Willson Peale, is a cherished feature of the Faculty Room today. The trustees paid for the portrait with a gift of 50 gold coins that had been presented to the college by Washington.

*B*enjamin Latrobe,
*America's first professional
architect, redesigned the gutted
Nassau Hall after the fire
of 1802. He replaced wooden
floors with brick and constructed a new sheet iron roof. This
lithograph by J.H. Bufford
was published in 1837.*

Nassau Hall still had not been completely repaired by the summer of 1783, when the Continental Congress moved temporarily from Philadelphia to Princeton to escape the wrath of disgruntled veterans demanding back pay. After initially meeting in Prospect, a stone farmhouse that was later replaced by the structure that became the home of the college president, Congress moved in early July to Nassau Hall, where it remained until early November. "The face of things inconceivably altered," wrote Ashbel Green, then a senior and later president of the college. "From a little obscure village we have become the capital of America."

The tiny village was unsuitable as a permanent home for Congress. Nonetheless, by the time Congress moved on in November 1783, Nassau Hall and the college at Princeton had become thoroughly associated in symbol and substance with the affairs of the United States. The college president, John

Witherspoon, had been a renowned advocate of independence. A disproportionate number of the leading lights in the Congress, who later became drafters of the Constitution and founding fathers of the United States, were graduates of Princeton.

The glory of Nassau Hall, however, soon gave way to troubled times. In March 1802 a disastrous fire broke out in the central belfry and was spread downward by high winds, leaving the building in ruins, with only its charred walls still standing. President Samuel Stanhope Smith blamed the disaster on arson by rebellious students infected with "vice and irreligion," but an independent investigation by a college senior indicated that the blaze was probably the fault of an incompetent chimney sweep.

An appeal for funds brought major contributions from citizens of six states and a hefty gift from friends at Harvard. This provided the money to rebuild Nassau Hall, with enough left over

Woodcut of the burning of Nassau Hall by Joseph Low, commissioned by the Princeton Print Club in the 1950s.

This 1860 lithograph shows the restoration by John Notman after the fire of 1855. The Italian Renaissance style was much in vogue at the time, accounting for the square towers at either end of the building. They were finally removed in 1905. Notman also designed Prospect and Lowrie House, the former and current presidential residences. Identifiable figures include President John Maclean (in top hat), Professor and Mrs. Henry Clay Cameron and Professor Lyman Atwater.

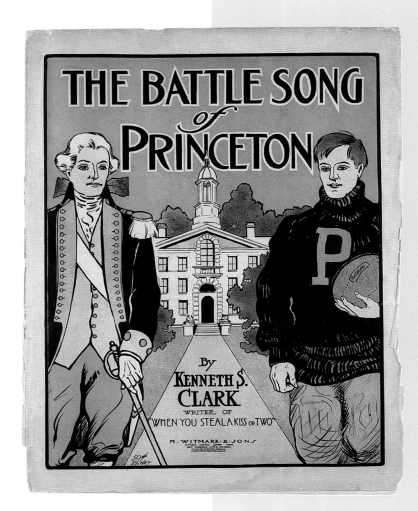

S*heet Music by Kenneth S. Clark '05. "When Princeton, old Princeton, first won her reknown, the rattle of battle was heard in the town. While they were scrapping, and John Bull was napping, our fore-fathers made a touchdown."*

to build the first two additional academic buildings a few yards away, one of which still stands as Stanhope Hall. The architect of the rebuilt Nassau Hall was Benjamin Henry Latrobe, who won greater fame as the chief architect of the U.S. Capitol in Washington.

In 1855 fire struck again, started by live embers falling from the grate of a student room on the second floor. Within minutes the building was a roaring furnace. Soon there was only a smoldering ruin between the massive stone walls. Once again, the trustees raised funds to restore the venerable building. This time they turned to a successful Philadelphia architect, John Notman, who employed low brick arches resting on iron rails for fireproofing. The worn brick floors and circular stairs familiar to later generations of Princetonians date from the post-1855 renovation. Notman raised the cupola to new heights, eliminated the entrance doors near the east and west ends of the north face, and added two prominent towers (later removed) at either end of the building in a bow to then-fashionable Italian Renaissance style.

In addition to these disasters, Nassau Hall endured recurrent student riots and rebellions. In the Great Rebellion of 1807, the most serious in Princeton's history, the faculty suspended 125 students—nearly three-fourths of the entire student body at that time—after they rebelled against disciplinary action taken against three of their number. After being dismissed, the rebels began locking doors and windows, barricading themselves in the building. They maintained a lengthy standoff before giving up their insurrection.

In another spectacular moment, troublemakers in 1814 detonated "the big cracker," two pounds of gunpowder in a hollow log. It blew away the central door of Nassau Hall and broke many windows. In 1817, in a famous incident, students protesting the length of assigned readings nailed up all entrances to the building and shouted false alarms of "Fire! Fire!" while incessantly ringing the bell in the central tower.

The bell, which tolled the beginning and end of classroom periods and the 9:00 p.m. curfew, became a recurrent object of student pranks. In 1864 a daring student climbed up the outside of the bell tower and made off with the clapper, making it necessary for a janitor to strike the bell with a hammer until a new clapper could be ordered and installed. Stealing the clapper later became a traditional freshman rite of honor, forcing the college, even in the 19th century, to keep a barrel of extra clappers on hand.

Late in the 20th century, in an age of liability lawsuits, the university became increasingly concerned about the danger involved in clapper-stealing. When a freshman armed with 13 pounds of tools fell from the outer wall of the bell tower in April 1992, plunging 40 feet to the ground,

A quartet of smiling Class of 1952 clapper thieves (l-r): James D. Sparkman, Jr., James P. Crutcher, Beveridge J. Rockefeller, Jr., and Jefferson C. Wright.

The mace presented by the community in 1956 on the 200th anniversary of the university's move to Princeton. It is carried by the faculty mace-bearer in major convocations.

President Harold Shapiro ordered the clapper removed, silencing the Nassau Hall bell. "Given the litigiousness of our age, we have no choice...," Shapiro announced "with special sadness." The following September, nevertheless, several freshmen were apprehended about 4:00 a.m. on the roof of Nassau Hall, telling proctors they were checking to see if the clapper was still there to be stolen.

Not surprisingly, in view of its importance, Nassau Hall has been the site of numerous protest demonstrations in recent decades on issues ranging from the deadly serious— U.S. bombing in Vietnam and university investment in South Africa—to the decidedly less earthshaking, as when a group of seniors dumped beer and wine bottles on the building's steps at midnight in September 1991 to demonstrate their disapproval of the university's ban on keg beer in rooms and new drinking restrictions at the eating clubs.

The Faculty Room, which is used today for meetings of the faculty and the trustees, contains portraits of all the previous presidents of Princeton and many of its founders and early benefactors. It also contains a symbolic mace that was presented to the university in 1956 by the Princeton community in appreciation of 200 years of mostly peaceful coexistence. The mace is carried by the faculty mace-bearer in official university convocations.

Since 1919 the entrance hall of Nassau Hall has been a memorial to all Princetonians who died in American wars, with their names inscribed on the walls. Facing the main entrance is a

*S*heet of Nassau Hall bicentennial three-cent stamps issued in 1956. The U.S. Government Printing Office used a 1776 engraving by New Haven artist Amos Doolittle as its model. Stamps from the first issue were purchased at the Princeton post office by a young philatelist.

Latin inscription by Dean West: Memoria Aeterna Retinet Alma Mater Filios Pro Patria Animas Ponentes (Alma Mater keeps in eternal memory her sons who laid down their lives for their country).

Today Nassau Hall stands solid and serene, a tangible reminder of the long history and strong traditions of the university it symbolizes. Older than the nation itself, it exudes a sense of the past that is equaled by few other buildings in the United States. In recognition of this, the U.S. government placed Nassau Hall on a postage stamp commemorating its bicentennial in 1956 and designated it a National Historic Landmark in 1960. But unlike Independence Hall in Philadelphia and many other historic sites, Nassau Hall to this day is in everyday use as the working center of an illustrious educational enterprise.

South Africa protest behind Nassau Hall, February 1978.

Bonfire on Cannon Green after 1994 football victories over Harvard and Yale, taken from the roof of Whig Hall.

Things Named After Princeton

A steroid Princetonia, number 508, discovered in 1903 by astronomy professor Raymond Dugan.

P hrygilus Princetonianus, a type of finch discovered in Cheike, Patagonia, in 1898.

C afe Princeton, in the town of Bobo Dioulasso, Burkina Faso, West Africa.

P rinceton Glacier, which flows into Nassau Fjord, an arm of Prince William Sound in southern Alaska. It was named in 1909 by George W. Perkins of the U.S. Coast and Geodetic Survey. This high-altitude color infrared photograph shows an area nine miles square.

Mt. Princeton, near Buena Vista, Colorado, was climbed and named in 1872 by a group of Princeton students on a summer field expedition. They were led by Harvard geology professor Joshua Dwight Whitney, after whom Mt. Whitney in the Sierra Nevada range is named. At 14,197 feet, Mt. Princeton is 223 feet shorter than Mt. Harvard but one foot taller than Mt. Yale.

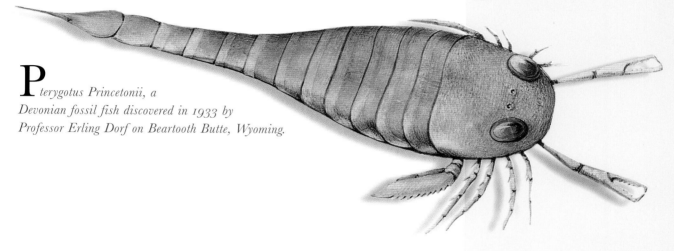

Pterygotus Princetonii, a Devonian fossil fish discovered in 1933 by Professor Erling Dorf on Beartooth Butte, Wyoming.

The "Princeton," a style of haircut that came into fashion in the 1950s and still has a following today. The cut is very short around the sides and just long enough on top to allow a part. In this 1956 photograph, Professor Robert Goheen '40 demonstrates the ideal Princeton cut.

Nassauica Dusenii, a plant first found in Patagonia in 1897.

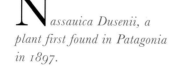

3

The Witherspoon Era

In August 1768 a Scottish minister named John Witherspoon, his wife and five children arrived in Philadelphia by boat from Glasgow. Greeted with enthusiasm by the local Presbyterian gentry, the Witherspoons set out by carriage for Princeton, where he was to take up his post as the sixth president of the College of New Jersey. A mile from town the Witherspoon entourage was met by the college's vice president, its three tutors and all 63 members of the student body. That night, in celebration, candles were lit in every window of Nassau Hall.

Before Witherspoon arrived, the presidency of the college had been held by five different men during its first 22 years. He kept the post for 26 years, longer than all his predecessors combined. Despite the trials of war and revolution, he strengthened the intellectual capital, reputation and finances of the fledgling college and, building on the inclinations of its founders, pointed it firmly in the direction of public service. This transplanted Scottish divine was a leading member of the Continental Congress and the only clergyman and only college president to sign the Declaration of Independence. After independence he contributed greatly to the organization of the national Presbyterian church, whose earlier schisms had given rise to the college, and preached the opening sermon to the church's first

General Assembly. In tribute to his versatility, Woodrow Wilson described Witherspoon as "a man so compounded of statesman and scholar, Calvinist, Scotsman and orator that it must ever

be a sore puzzle where to place or rank him—whether among the great divines, great teachers, or great statesmen."

Witherspoon's period of intense concentration on college affairs lasted for only about one-third of his administration, from its onset to the outbreak of the Revolutionary War, after which he was often diverted by affairs of state and church and eventually by blindness. Nevertheless, Witherspoon set the course for the future Princeton University to a remarkable degree. He was, by all accounts, Princeton's first great president.

❦

John Witherspoon was born in 1723, the son of a minister of the Church of Scotland, at that time probably the most enlightened part of the Protestant church. He graduated from the University of Edinburgh and made a reputation as a teacher, scholar and churchman, which brought him to the attention of Princeton's trustees when they were searching for a new president for the troubled college. Witherspoon himself was ready for a new life in the new world, but his wife was reluctant. He turned down the presidency when it was first offered to him and accepted only when his wife was persuaded by Princeton's emissaries to change her mind.

At the time of Witherspoon's arrival, the college that had been launched with such enthusiasm 22 years earlier had come upon hard times, partly because of its dizzying turnover at the top. Its first president, Jonathan Dickinson, had died within a year of

Oil painting of John Witherspoon by Charles Willson Peale, circa 1787. Peale had to send Witherspoon at least two polite dunning letters to receive payment for this portrait, an indication of the college's severe financial straits. Witherspoon accepted the presidency after two future signers of the Declaration of Independence, Richard Stockton, Class of 1748, and Benjamin Rush, Class of 1760, visited him at his home in Paisley, Scotland, following the death of Samuel Finley.

Richard Stockton

*R*ichard Stockton was the
only one in the first class of
six students to graduate from
Princeton (1748) who did not
become a cleric. A signer of the
Declaration of Independence,
Stockton fled from Princeton in
the fall of 1776. Several months
later he returned an ill man. He
found his home pillaged, his
wealth lost, and this portrait
slashed by the Hessians. Stockton
remained an impoverished invalid
until his death in 1781.

*B*ronze medallion commemorating the 150th anniversary of
the Declaration of Independence
depicts Princeton's three signers
(l-r): Richard Stockton, Class
of 1748; Benjamin Rush, 1760;
and President John Witherspoon.

taking office. His successor, Aaron Burr, Sr., had moved the college to its permanent home in Princeton and built Nassau Hall,
but he died at age 41 after 10 years in office. The third president,
the eminent philosopher-theologian Jonathan Edwards, had died
only six weeks after taking office. The fourth, Samuel Davies, had
lasted only 18 months before dying. The fifth president, Samuel
Finley, had lasted five years but had been unable to put the college on its feet.

Witherspoon's inaugural address as Princeton's president,
declaimed in Latin at commencement exercises in September
1768, was on "the Connection & mutual influences of Learning
& Piety." The two subjects and their relationship were of crucial
importance in the Witherspoon era. The initial emphasis of the
college had been on piety, although from the beginning the
founders intended to train students for the state as well as the
church. To the surprise of some who summoned him from
Scotland because of his fame as a cleric, Witherspoon broadened
the institution's educational philosophy, giving greater emphasis
to the humanities and science. He saw no contradiction between
faith and reason; he preached from the pulpit twice each Sunday
and during the week taught history, rhetoric and French as well
as "moral philosophy." He was a devotee of the scientific method
of testing theory by experience and firmly believed in common
sense as the test of any proposition.

By precept and example Witherspoon created the model
of "Princeton in the Nation's Service" later proclaimed by
Wilson. His students included, in addition to a U.S. president
(James Madison) and vice president (Aaron Burr, Jr.), 10 cabinet
officers, 21 senators, 39 members of the House of
Representatives, three justices of the Supreme Court and 12 state
governors. The 55 members of the Constitutional Convention of
1787, the founding fathers of the United States, included nine

Princeton graduates, more than from any other college in the colonies or abroad, of whom five had been students of Witherspoon. The guiding hand of the convention was Madison, one of Witherspoon's star pupils, who, by remaining to study for a year after graduating in 1771, may have been Princeton's first nontheological graduate student.

Witherspoon's accomplishments did not come easily. When he arrived, the college was nearly bankrupt. He quickly undertook extensive travels to raise money and to extol the virtues of the college, preaching at many prominent churches as well as backwater locations from Boston to Virginia. Gradually the college was placed on a firm financial footing, only to face potential ruin again a few years later as a result of the severe damage to Nassau Hall in the Revolutionary War and the college's unwise investment in government bonds. The penniless

Annis Boudinot Stockton

UNTIL COEDUCATION, ONLY WOMAN EVER ELECTED TO WHIG MEMBERSHIP

Annis Boudinot Stockton, Richard's wife, was mother of two Princeton sons, sister of Elias Boudinot, president of the Continental Congress, and mother-in-law to Benjamin Rush. She was a poet who named her husband's family estate "Morven" after the mythical Kingdom of Fingal. Before the Battle of Princeton, Annis hid some of the college's most valuable artifacts from the British, along with important state papers. For these services she was elected posthumously to Whig Hall in 1876, the first woman member. Annis penned a yearly ode to her husband on the anniversary of his death. She survived him for 20 years, dying in 1801.

Limited edition Wedgewood plate showing Witherspoon Hall, manufactured in 1930.

Continental Congress, over Witherspoon's objection, refused to support its bonded indebtedness. But by then the fame of the college and of its president, and their association with the future of the young nation, helped Princeton weather the financial storm.

At the college's start, as was common in those days, the principal admission requirements and course of study emphasized the Latin and Greek classics. A 1774 letter from a Princeton undergraduate to his brother who hoped to enter the junior class explained, "The studies you will be examined on...are Virgil, Horace, Cicero's Orations, Lucian, Xenophon, Homer, geography and logic.... Try to accustom yourself to read Greek and Latin well as it is much looked to here and be accurate in geography." Mathematics and philosophy were well established. With the spirit of scientific inquiry spreading from Europe, Witherspoon placed a growing emphasis on physics, chemistry, mathematics and astronomy.

Witherspoon brought with him from Scotland his personal library of 300 volumes, which he contributed to the college shelves, and he consistently ordered more books, with special emphasis on works in English. When he learned that David Rittenhouse, a renowned Philadelphia scientist, had created a mechanical replica of the movement of the planets called an orrery, Witherspoon rode to Rittenhouse's home and purchased the delicate mechanism for £220. This was an extraordinary expenditure at a time when the yearly tuition was £5 per student and the annual budget of the college was less than £2,000. The orrery, an 18th-century forerunner of a planetarium, was considered a marvel of the age when installed in Nassau Hall.

During Witherspoon's presidency the college grounds were the ·flat and tree-lined acres originally contributed by

Benjamin Rush

A LEADING PATRIOT AND THE "FATHER OF AMERICAN PSYCHIATRY"

*D*r. *Benjamin Rush (opposite), Class of 1760, signed the Declaration of Independence, treated the wounded at the Battle of Princeton, served in the Continental Congress, campaigned vigorously for the abolition of slavery, pressed for improvements in women's education, trained more than 3,000 medical students, ran the U.S. Mint, instigated the American temperance movement, founded an infirmary for the poor, and dramatically advanced the treatment for mental illness. He became known as the "Father of American Psychiatry."*

*R*ush's *"Tranquillizer," 1810. "I am about to introduce a chair into our Hospital to keep the maniacs in the inflammatory stage of their disease in a perpendicular position so as to save the head from the impetus of the blood as much as possible."*

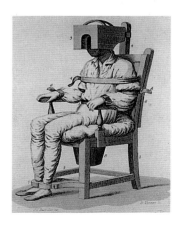

MADISON

Nathaniel FitzRandolph, with the only buildings being Nassau Hall and the adjacent President's House. Princeton's pastoral setting apparently was a surprise to Witherspoon, who was accustomed to city universities in Scotland. Witherspoon is credited by etymologists with first applying the word "campus" (which is Latin for field) to the college setting rather than calling it a yard, as was usual then. His description stuck, and gradually the word campus was adopted by universities throughout the country, with the notable exception of Harvard Yard.

Dealing with students in a revolutionary age was not easy, and the college was beset by instances of disorder and rebellion. Looking out from beneath his bushy brows and speaking in a Scottish burr that never left him, Witherspoon took it all calmly. His advice to his tutors was that they should "govern always, but beware of governing too much. Convince your pupils...that you would rather gratify than thwart them; that you wish to see them happy, and desire to impose no restraints but such as their real advantage and the order of the college render indispensable. Put a wide difference between youthful follies and foibles, and those acts which manifest a malignant spirit, and an intentional insubordination."

As the revolution approached, both Witherspoon and the college he led were increasingly caught up in the epochal struggle around them. Although a newcomer to the new world, Witherspoon, as a disciple of the political freedoms endorsed by the Scottish enlightenment, was a strong advocate of independence. John Adams, stopping in Princeton on his way to the first meeting of the Continental Congress, called on Witherspoon and declared him to be "as high a Son of Liberty as any Man in America."

When New Jersey began to organize against the British in 1774, Witherspoon quickly became a leader in the cause and wrote many pro-independence articles and sermons. He was selected in 1776 as a New Jersey delegate to the Continental Congress, where he advocated and signed the Declaration of Independence. After war broke out Witherspoon called the students together to announce the approach of British troops to Princeton. The students gathered their belongings and said hasty good-byes to one another and to their professors. Witherspoon loaded a few valued possessions in a wagon and left on horseback for Pennsylvania.

After the Battle of Princeton, a handful of students returned to a devastated campus in the summer of 1777 to resume their studies. With Nassau Hall uninhabitable, they were lodged and fed in town and assembled for their classes in the President's House, often under the instruction of Witherspoon himself, until the damage was repaired.

Increasingly, though, Witherspoon was diverted by the affairs of the Congress, where he served as one of its busiest and most influential members until he retired from political life in 1782. While in Congress, Witherspoon served on at least 100 committees, including the Board of War, which was responsible for military affairs, and the Committee on Secret Correspondence, which originated American diplomacy. He was a major figure in devising the Articles of Confederation and helped organize the U.S. executive departments. As a commuter between classes in Princeton and Congress in

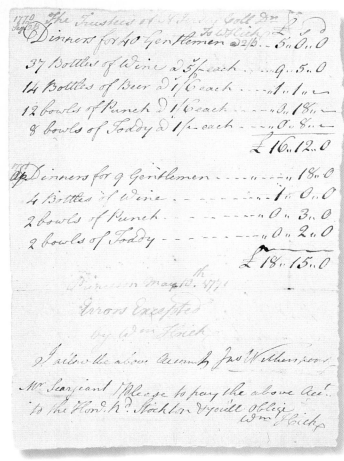

Bill for two trustees' dinners in 1770 and 1771.

Witherspoon's glass decanter, from Firestone Library's 18th-century room.

D r. Harry Ashworth, a research associate in the department of Aeronautical Engineering, restored the orrery after World War II.

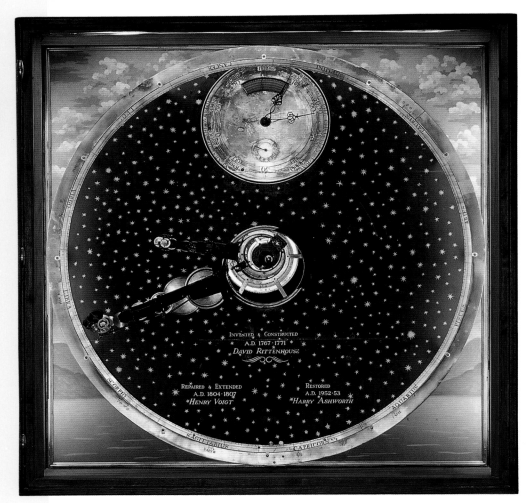

The Orrery

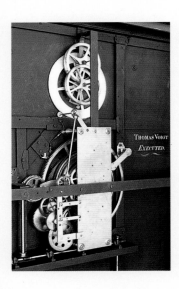

The Rittenhouse Orrery, purchased by John Witherspoon in 1771, was like a miniature planetarium showing the relative positions and motions of the planets and their moons. After having been well-guarded during the British occupation of Nassau Hall, the orrery was badly damaged by troops of the Continental Army. It was finally repaired, but only partially, between 1804 and 1807. After another long period of neglect, it was dusted off and sent to the World's Columbian Exposition in Chicago in 1893, after which it was inexplicably lost for more than half a century despite recurrent attempts to locate it. It was accidentally rediscovered in the summer of 1948, when workmen in the carpenters' shop in the basement of McCosh Hall summoned Professor Newton L. Pierce of the Astronomy department to look at a box of instruments that seemed "slightly astronomical" among old packing cases about to be discarded. The famous orrery was still in its shipping box from the Chicago fair. The instrument was returned to working order by Harry Ashworth and is displayed today in Peyton Hall, the headquarters of the Astrophysics department.

Philadelphia, he was a familiar figure on horseback on the New Jersey and Pennsylvania roads.

In 1779, with the affairs of the infant nation pressing Witherspoon, the need was clear for a strong second-in-command who could help to administer the college's affairs as well as teach. The trustees chose Witherspoon's son-in-law, Samuel Stanhope Smith of the Class of 1769, who had gone on to preach in Virginia and to play a leading role in the founding of two academies that later became Hampden-Sydney College and Washington and Lee University. Witherspoon turned over to Smith much of the daily administrative and teaching burden as well as one-half of his presidential salary of £400 and the President's House. Witherspoon moved to Tusculum, his farm a mile north of the campus.

Witherspoon resigned from Congress in 1782 and began to turn his attention back to classes, riding over from

As president of Princeton (1812-22), Ashbel Green devoted much of his time to raising money for the theological seminary, founded in 1812, while his own college verged on financial collapse.

Sketch of Witherspoon's farm, Tusculum, from The Princeton Book *of 1879.*

Tusculum regularly to take charge of the seniors. But the following year the political arena came to him when Congress made its unexpected move from Philadelphia to Princeton.

With Witherspoon presiding, the commencement ceremony of September 1783 was probably the most star-studded event of any college occasion in American history. Gathered in the Presbyterian church at the edge of the campus with the senior class, other students, and faculty were George Washington, who had recently been received by Congress in Nassau Hall in formal appreciation for his wartime leadership, the ministers of France and Holland, seven signers of the Declaration of Independence, nine signers of the Articles of Confederation, 11 future signers of the Constitution of the United States and many members of Congress. Before this august crowd the valedictorian, Ashbel Green, later president of Princeton, praised Washington in ringing phrases, and seniors debated such questions as "Was Brutus justified in killing Caesar?" and "Can any measure that is morally evil be politically good?" A British officer, eavesdropping on the occasion to gauge colonial sentiment, was appalled at the "farce" he observed and described Witherspoon as a "political firebrand, who perhaps had not a less share in the Revolution than Washington himself." The college president, he wrote in his report,

Samuel Stanhope Smith, Class of 1769, the first alumnus to serve as president (1795-1812), was a fine administrator, a brilliant academician and a beloved personality, but his tenure was marred by many unfortunate incidents, including the suspicious burning of Nassau Hall and a number of student insurrections. Many trustees lost patience with the students, and a severe conflict developed between a meddlesome board and an increasingly rebellious student body.

"poisons the minds of his young students and through them the Continent."

Due to the ill feeling generated in Britain by the drive for colonial independence and the Revolutionary War, Witherspoon's fund-raising trip to London shortly after the 1783 commencement produced little revenue for the college. A shipboard accident, moreover, cost Witherspoon the use of one of his eyes and led in time to the nearly total blindness that afflicted his later years. Witherspoon's wife died in 1789, and two years later he married a 24-year-old widow, an occasion enthusiastically celebrated by Princeton students with the firing of cannons, music by a student orchestra and the illumination of Nassau Hall by even more candles than greeted his original arrival on the campus.

With blindness creeping up on him, "the Old Doctor," as he became known, was increasingly remote from the daily life of the college. Still president of Princeton, he died in 1794 at his farm at Tusculum.

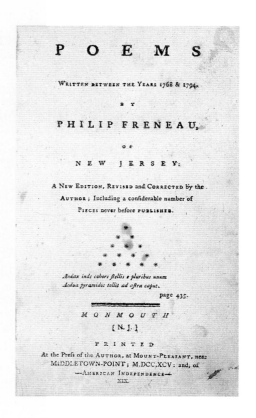

Philip Freneau, Class of 1771, was known as the "Poet of the Revolution."

An oddly different view of Witherspoon featuring his famed bushy brows, drawn from life and engraved in 1785.

There are two kinds of speaking that are very interesting...perfect sense and perfect nonsense. When there is speaking in either of these ways I shall engage to be all attention. But when there is speaking, as there often is, halfway between sense and nonsense, you must bear with me if I fall asleep.

JOHN WITHERSPOON

Early 19th-Century Princeton: A Period of Eclipse

The 67-year span between John Witherspoon's death and the Civil War marked a long period of eclipse in Princeton's history. Student unrest, religious divisions, financial difficulties and declining enrollment brought the college to the brink of extinction.

Despite his nickname, President James "Boss" Carnahan was a timid leader who had neither the vision nor the energy to turn the college around. That difficult task was taken up by Professor John Maclean, Jr., Class of 1816. Named vice president, he persuaded Carnahan and the trustees to strengthen the faculty, improve student living conditions, and establish the highly effective Alumni Association of Nassau Hall.

James Carnahan, Class of 1800, served Princeton longer than any other president, from 1823 to 1854. During the early years of his presidency, enrollment declined from 148 to 66 before the college began to turn around under the leadership of Carnahan's vice president, Professor John Maclean, Jr., who later succeeded him as president.

Perhaps the greatest American scientist of the 19th century, Joseph Henry served on the Princeton faculty from 1832 to 1846. He left to become the first secretary of the Smithsonian Institution. He built this telegraphic receiver (above), and installed the world's first telegraph line to signal from his laboratory to his home that he was ready for lunch.

In 1844 Henry was asked to investigate a disastrous cannon explosion aboard the U.S.S. Princeton, the most technologically advanced warship of its day and the first naval vessel to employ a screw propeller. The explosion had killed the Secretary of State, the Secretary of the Navy and several members of Congress. Henry's investigation of the gun casing led him to study the molecular cohesion of matter.

Leonard Jerome (below, left), Class of 1840, one of Princeton's legendary student pranksters, organized more than 100 undergraduates to haul a Revolutionary War cannon to campus in 1838 and deposit it in front of Nassau Hall. Two years later it was buried in the middle of Cannon Green. Jerome went on to make a fortune on Wall Street. His daughter was the mother of Winston Churchill; Lady Sarah Churchill, Winston's daughter, is shown with the cannon.

Henry built this globe with current-carrying wires wrapped in a spiral as a model of the earth's magnetic field. He used it as a teaching device for his students. Henry's chief scientific contributions were in the field of electromagnetism, where he discovered the phenomenon of self-inductance. The unit of inductance, called the "henry," immortalizes his name.

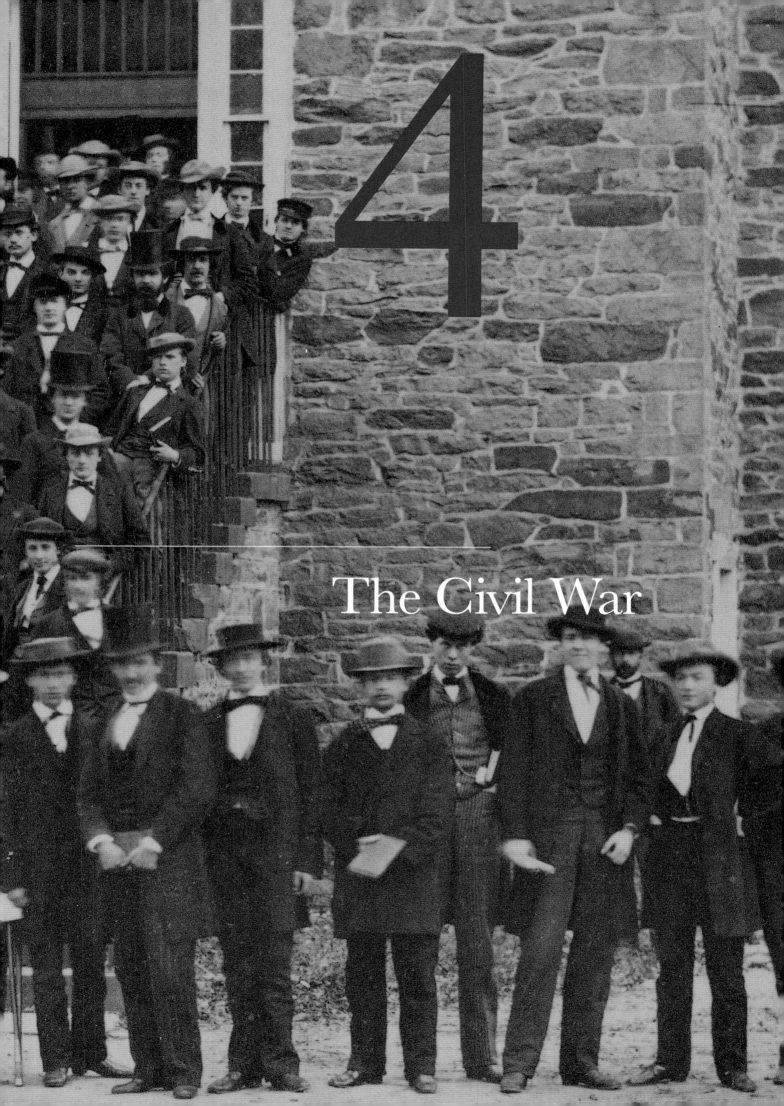

4

The Civil War

19th-*century watch fobs worn by members of Whig and Clio. Whig had been born in 1769 and Clio in 1770.*

Under President Witherspoon Princeton had educated many influential Southerners. As the Civil War approached, it had become known as a popular Northern haven for students from the South, a reputation it maintained into the post-World War II era. By 1860, the year of Lincoln's election to the presidency and the eve of the outbreak of war, Princeton had grown to 314 students, nearly one-third of whom were from south of the Mason-Dixon line.

Many of the Southern students were confident and prosperous, well schooled in the ways of friendship as well as literary and scholastic skills. "These boys were liked by their fellow classmen, took a prominent part in college life and gave to the institution a decidedly southern flavor," according to bicentennial historian Thomas Jefferson Wertenbaker. On the Princeton campus, where residential life made for close friendships among those from disparate origins, it was with particular anguish that ties were abruptly severed in the sectional strife that tore apart the nation.

❦

Earlier in the 19th century, in a period described by Wertenbaker and other historians as Princeton's lowest ebb, the college had been shaken by riots, rebellions and disastrous fires. Extracurricular life increasingly revolved around the two great literary and debating clubs, the American Whig Society and the rival Cliosophic Society, which had constructed their own Greek-style temples of stucco and wood behind Nassau Hall in 1838 (later replaced by the marble halls that still stand today).

By the 1860s the college had recovered its equilibrium and vitality, due in large part to a rescue effort by loyal alumni, who had first organized as an alumni association in 1826 with James Madison as president. At this point, however, the national contro-

*P*opular postcard of cherub cheering out the Princeton locomotive, printed in 1909. This signature salute dates from the Civil War era. It was originally adapted from the New York Seventh Regiment "skyrocket," which the troops shouted to students as they passed through the Princeton train depot on their way to war. While the tiger was not yet universally associated with Princeton in the 1860s, its identification as Princeton's mascot had begun.

*T*he Cloaca Maxima, built in 1861 and nestled between the old Whig and Clio buildings, was the college's main sanitary facility. With its discreet Latin moniker, even it displayed a touch of the classical. Unlike its flimsy wooden predecessors, the stone and brick Cloaca was fireproof at a time when outhouse burning was a favorite student pastime.

versy over slavery spread to the campus with powerful effect. In contrast to the strong abolitionist sentiment at New England colleges, defenders of slavery were influential and outspoken at Princeton. Records suggest that prior to the Civil War, defenders of the status quo usually won the frequent debates on the subject, victories that were undoubtedly based on campus sentiment as well as oratorical skill.

John DeWitt of the Class of 1861, later a Princeton trustee, recalled that "political talk was frequent and exciting on the campus, in the dormitories and in the Halls [the Whig and Clio debating societies]. Its central and persistent theme was slavery: and this was discussed from every point of view; its relations to the Bible, to the Federal Constitution, to society, and to economics." At the same time, though, DeWitt also observed that despite increasingly sharp political disagreements on the campus, "as if anticipating their end, friendships became even closer than ever."

In December 1859 Southern students led a march up Nassau Street protesting John Brown's raid and abolitionist activity. Edward Burrows, a student from Mississippi, wrote his sister Kate at home that "I think probably there will be some

hot times here if an abolitionist is elected next president."
With the election of Abraham Lincoln in 1860,
his prophecy was fulfilled. As the
Southern states seceded late
that year and early the following year, emotions
rose on the campus as
well as in the nation,
and Southern stu-
dents began leaving
the campus to return
home to fight.

Usually the Southerners
left in groups of 10 to 20, and they were
often escorted to the train station in a good-bye procession of
their Northern friends. "As the trains came in sight came also the
tears," recalled a witness of these sad farewells. Classmates and
college friends were well aware that they might never meet
again, or only on opposite sides of the battle lines where soldiers
would kill or be killed.

As the tension mounted sharply with the Confederate
attack on Fort Sumter, a group of Northern students raised the
stars and stripes over Nassau Hall. The flag was quickly removed
on the order of President John Maclean, who feared it would
touch off unnecessary conflicts among the students. The decision to remove the flag was widely condemned in newspapers of
the North, and Northern students were upset. A student committee was organized to formally place the colors back on
Nassau Hall. This time the administration acquiesced.

Shortly before the ceremony, according to the Class of
1861's DeWitt, a representative of the remaining Southern students asked that they be permitted to join in a final ceremony to

1860 *Nassau
Baseball Club, posing on
a ball field where the Art
Museum now stands, with
Prospect in the background.
Organized sports began to
appear on campus in the late
1850s, but this is the earliest
team portrait in the history of
Princeton athletics. The 1860
Nassau nine played the college's first "away" game, fit-
tingly, in the city of Orange,
New Jersey. The game was
called on account of darkness
with the score tied at 42 all.*

AT ARLINGTON, VA., THE HEADQUARTERS OF GENERAL RUNYON'S NEW JERSEY BRIGADE.

Camp Princeton of the New Jersey Brigade in Arlington, Virginia. This encampment was made in July 1861 just before the Battle of Bull Run. It was probably named by New Jersey Governor Charles Olden, who also served as Princeton College's treasurer.

salute the national flag. The parade to Nassau Hall was headed by a Southern student, John Dawson of Canton, Mississippi, who played his fiddle to accompany the singing of the "Star-Spangled Banner." For most of the remaining Southern students, "This was to be their farewell," wrote DeWitt. "The flag was raised. The salute was given. The Southern students—not many, for most had hastened home—then marched off the campus, the Northern students standing uncovered before them at salute. Before the next day the most of them were gone." By April 23, 1861, 11 days after the war began, most of the Southern students had been given permission to withdraw on honorable terms from college "in consequence of the state of the country."

In a widely publicized incident the following September, a Brooklyn-born student who had expressed sympathy for the secession was dragged from his bed and held under the college water

pump in back of Nassau Hall. Maclean and the faculty, reacting once more against unauthorized action that they feared might divide the campus, suspended the three students who had led the hazing. This misjudgment of the tenor of the times made the three suspended students heroes in the eyes of their college mates and townspeople. "Both town and college were subjected to an excitement such as Princeton probably never before had felt," recalled Clay MacCauley, Class of 1864, who had just returned to the campus after service in the Union army. MacCauley felt that with this emotional incident, the tide of opinion had turned. Following a gala procession through town, the three martyrs rode in honor in a flag-draped carriage to the train station amid the cheers of a large crowd. "No one who saw that shouting crowd of college boys marching slowly to fife and drum music through Princeton's main street, cheered on by the waving hands and banners, and the 'applause of all Princeton,' could ever forget the sight," wrote MacCauley years afterward. All three suspended students later served in the Union army.

Of the 88 students in the Class of 1861 who began their senior year in the autumn of 1860, only 45 were still in school to take final examinations in the spring. Twenty from the class served in the Union army, of whom five were killed, and 21 in the Confederate army, of whom four were killed. The Class of 1862

Brigadier General James J. Archer, Class of 1835 (top), served in every battle of the Army of Northern Virginia before he was captured at Gettysburg. Brigadier General Lawrence O'Brian Branch, Class of 1838, was a North Carolina congressman before joining the Confederate army. He was killed by a sharp-shooter's bullet at Antietam.

Francis DuBoise, Jr., Class of 1863, was placed under the college pump where "that venerable institution was put into operation and continued to pour forth its aqueous contents until the fire of disunion was pretty well quenched in his breast." This sketch of the three heroes of the "pumping" incident being triumphally escorted from town was made at the time of the event.

As Ewing Graham McClure, Class of 1862, of Tennessee prepared to leave Princeton in his junior year to fight for the Confederacy, he purchased a leather-bound autograph book and passed it among his friends and classmates from North and South alike. Such autograph books were common in the mid-19th century, but this one—which was uncovered by his family more than a century later—provides an extraordinary glimpse of sentiments among Princeton students as the war began early in 1861.

"Mac" McClure, as he was nicknamed, was 23 years old at the time. Tall and auburn-haired, he had been active in Whig Hall. Here are some of the messages in his book:

McClure's Autograph Book

Dear Mac:

It is with feelings of sorrow that I see you and my many other friends from the noble old State of Tennessee so abruptly departing from among us. I had hoped the difficulties that so long threatened our now distraught country might be amicably settled, but alas, they have not, and war now reigns throughout our land. I shall hope however that you will not allow this to interfere with the memory of those whom you leave here. I have ever had the highest esteem for you and all the rest of your fellow statesmen and I can assure you that come what may, the memory of the halcyon days of college shall never be eradicated, or disturbed. You go to defend your own state and I shall endeavor, if called upon, to do the same for mine. Hoping that I may be kindly remembered by you, I am very happy in signing myself

Your friend and classmate
John Cochran
New Jersey

My dear Mac:

The last goodbye will soon be said and you will be on your way to your native state, which I saw in a telegram yesterday was a unit for the Union two days ago and unless they are very fickle must still be so. Be it so, may the star spangled banner long wave over the whole Union and may Tennessee do her share to support the government. If however Tennessee secedes as the played-out Secessionists hope, and you become a soldier, don't shoot down if you see in the ranks, any old friends and least of all

Your friend and classmate
Charles E. Webster
Mauch Chunk, Penn. U.S.A.

Dear Mac:

Our friendship as classmates has been firm and true and it is with feelings of deep regret that I write these parting words. God only knows the result of this awful struggle in our country. Oh that North and South might again be friends even though as two countries! God bless you, my classmate, tho' those who know the union, the love, the sympathy which has bound our class together alone can know my feelings as I pen these few lines. You know my heart and what I would say if I had the time. Ever remember me kindly and may we meet in Heaven where war is no more.

Your classmate and true friend
Lewis W. Mudge
New York

McClure served in the Confederate army as a captain. After the war he returned to his farm in Washington County, Tennessee, and reopened the local Washington College Academy. He lived to the age of 71 and is buried in a cemetery adjoining the academy's campus.

Daguerrotype of Professor John Maclean, Jr., Class of 1816, circa 1844. He became president of Princeton in 1854.

Envelope from Abraham Lincoln's handwritten letter accepting his Princeton honorary degree, December 20, 1864. It was only the third such degree—and the last— that he would receive. The letter is an excellent example of Lincoln's concise prose style, and is one of the university's most valued treasures. Lincoln wrote that he was "thankful if my labors have seemed to conduce to the preservation of those institutions under which alone we can expect good government and in its train sound learning and the progress of the liberal arts." Lincoln's signature served as a stamp because of his executive franking privilege.

dwindled from 81 in its prewar sophomore year to 53 by commencement, with most of the rest serving in one of the opposing armies.

In all Princeton contributed at least eight generals to the Confederacy and four generals to the Union. A large but uncountable number of lesser officers and enlisted men from Princeton served both sides. The War Memorial in Nassau Hall lists 70 Princetonians as having died in the Civil War. The plaque gives no sign and makes no distinction between those on the opposing sides. To this day student guides inform visitors to the campus that 35 died fighting for the North, and 35 died fighting for the South.

Once the Southerners had departed, campus sentiment turned sharply to the Union side for the rest of the war. Classes were canceled, and there was a huge bonfire of celebration on Cannon Green when Richmond was taken. Nonetheless, Princeton's historical Southern ties and the highly publicized 1861 episodes left a lingering impression of Confederate sympathy. To combat this perception, the

trustees in December 1864 bestowed an honorary degree on President Lincoln, who accepted in a handwritten letter in gratitude "that the course of the Government which I represent has received the approval of a body of gentlemen of such character and intelligence in this time of public trial...."

The college also arranged for delivery of a strongly patriotic commencement address in 1866, following the end of the war. This was prompted by a letter to President Maclean from S.H. Pennington, Sr., Class of 1825, reporting that "you gentlemen at

Jimmy
Johnson

**A BELOVED INSTITUTION ON
CAMPUS FOR GENERATIONS OF
PRINCETON STUDENTS**

Jimmy Johnson was a fugitive slave from Maryland who determined to seek his freedom after a friend and fellow slave, Frederick Douglass, successfully escaped. Johnson made it as far as Princeton, where he was captured in 1839. Theodosia Prevost, a descendant of John Witherspoon, negotiated to buy his freedom for $550. Princeton students took up a collection and paid a large share of his ransom.

Johnson worked on campus selling fruits, candies and lemonade for the next 60 years. He paid back every penny laid out for his freedom. He became a beloved institution to generations of Princetonians and a financial contributor to the college.

Behind him is a portraitist's painted backdrop of the campus depicting the old chapel and an image of Jimmy himself with his baskets of refreshments.

Princeton, in your comparative seclusion,...have very little idea of the extent of the distrust which has arisen in the minds of alumni and others, in consequence of occurrences in the College during the rebellion, and the alleged absence of patriotic demonstrations there on public occasions."

As the war receded into the past, the Princeton family sought to bind up its wounds. At the 10th reunion of the Class of 1856 immediately after the end of the conflict, the class secretary, reporting on the impact of the war, declared that all those who served the Union stand in "unalterable hostility to those principles whose armed supporters have been overthrown, [yet] they as freely disclaim any personal enmity to the men of the South, and offer nothing but friendship to Classmates." The Class of 1859, which contributed 15 fighters for the Union and 20 for the Confederacy, began a painstaking postwar effort to communicate with its Southern veterans. Some were reported dead. At least one had fled to Honduras. One classmate replied that due to the privations of every kind he had suffered, he had been at first unable to revive old friendships in the North, which had seemed to him "a foreign land." D.W. Moore, a classmate from Arkansas, wrote the class secretary four years after the war's end:

"I was not what we call an original secessionist, yet from the commencement of the open hostilities to the close of the war my interest in and devotion to the cause of the Confederacy never varied. Yet whatever our feelings and actions were then, and however much we may have differed, they are with the things of the past, and now the kindest recollections & good wishes should be cherished for each other...."

P rankish groups like the Trilobites, pictured here in 1871, began to appear as the gloom of civil war finally lifted. Below: Campus broadside celebrating the end of the war. "Flags flying, handkerchiefs waving, windows blazing, torchlights burning, fireworks flying through the air, everyone shouting, horns sounding—who ever beheld such a time in the usually quiet, serene Princeton!"

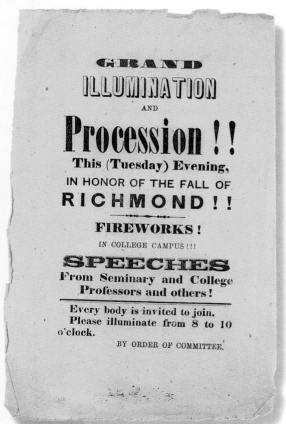

GRAND ILLUMINATION AND Procession !! This (Tuesday) Evening, IN HONOR OF THE FALL OF RICHMOND !! FIREWORKS ! IN COLLEGE CAMPUS !!! SPEECHES From Seminary and College Professors and others ! Every body is invited to join. Please illuminate from 8 to 10 o'clock. BY ORDER OF COMMITTEE.

The Princeton Tiger

The tiger emerged as Princeton's totem in the early 1880s because of the college's cheer, which employed "tiger, tiger tiger" as a rallying cry, and the growing use of orange and black. The colors were initially adopted by the Class of 1869 Base Ball Club, who as sophomores took on Yale in New Haven while sporting orange ribbons with black lettering that read: '69 B.B.C.

Princeton's first tiger, a cub, lept from the front cover of the inaugural edition of *Tiger Magazine* in 1882. In 1902 a pair of marble tigers holding shields appeared on the posts of the McCosh Walk gateway north of Little Hall. These sentries were the first free-standing tigers on campus.

For some in the late 19th century, the lion, which appears on the royal House of Nassau's coat of arms, seemed a more suitable beast, and bronze lions were installed at the entrance to Nassau Hall by the class of 1879 at its commencement. In 1911 the class replaced the lions with the Proctor tigers that stand guard to this day.

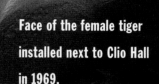

Face of the female tiger installed next to Clio Hall in 1969.

S*culptor Gutzon Borglum created this tiger and monkey gargoyle on the archway through 1879 Hall in 1904. Borglum later sculpted the presidential faces on Mount Rushmore.*

I*n 1985 the tigers at the entrance to Nassau Hall (left) were festooned with wreaths and balloons to celebrate Communiversity, an annual festival that brings together town and gown. "Our lofty elms so gently break The twilight crescent moon's soft light; Old Nassau's tigers slow awake: The seniors hold the steps tonight." (Step song by Ernest Carter, Class of 1888.)*

I*n 1923 the father of football player Albert (Red) Howard '25 captured a live tiger in India and brought it to Princeton as a mascot. It made the game crowds nervous and was soon given to a zoo.*

5

The McCosh Era

James McCosh and his faculty (previous page) outside the President's House (now Maclean House) in 1870. On the porch are (l-r) John T. Duffield, Lyman H. Atwater, McCosh, Stephen Alexander and Arnold H. Guyot. Standing on the ground are Henry C. Cameron, James C. Welling, John S. Schanck, Charles W. Shields, William A. Packard and Joseph Kargé.

PR.9   PRESIDENT'S RESIDENCE, PRINCETON UNIVERSITY, PRINCETON, N. J.

Prospect was given to Princeton in 1878 by two wealthy Scottish-American merchants, Alexander and Robert Stuart, for use as the president's home. McCosh vowed to open the house to students, and he faithfully kept that promise. "Many an alumnus cherished in his memory...that tea-table, a few students around it, the Doctor at the head, leading the conversation with his strong, cheery voice and slight Scotch accent; his wife Isabella, 'the mother of the students,' opposite him, pouring tea."

As the train pulled into the Princeton station, the waiting student body let forth a mighty cheer and then formed a triumphant procession to the President's House, where they gathered in a semicircle to be introduced formally to their new leader, a tall, round-shouldered, white-haired educator from Scotland. The time was October 1868, almost exactly 100 years after John Witherspoon, another renowned and energetic Scottish minister, had arrived to rescue Princeton from doldrums and make an indelible mark on the institution.

James McCosh arrived at a college of 20 faculty members and 288 students, notably fewer than before the school and the nation suffered the trauma of the Civil War. He retired nearly 20 years later, having more than doubled the rolls of teachers and students and having expanded the campus in a surge of building that reached for the first time beyond the immediate environs of Nassau Hall.

McCosh broadened Princeton's horizons, recruited a distinguished faculty and broke away from the lethargy that had settled on the college after the war. Woodrow Wilson, who was a Princeton undergraduate in the McCosh era, wrote of his former teacher, "He found Princeton a quiet country college and lifted it to a conspicuous place among the most notable institutions of the country.... He laid the foundations of a genuine university, and his own enthusiasm for learning vivified the whole spirit of the place."

❧

Jimmy McCosh, as he was affectionately known, was professor of logic and metaphysics at Queen's College, Belfast. He was known

He found Princeton a quiet country college and lifted it to a conspicuous place among the most notable institutions of the country....

WOODROW WILSON ABOUT MCCOSH

throughout the English-speaking world for his writings and his part in establishing the Free Church of Scotland, an evangelical offshoot of the established Scottish ministry. He was picked to be Princeton's president for much the same reason as Witherspoon a century before him: he was an eminent ecclesiastical figure from afar without ties to any American faction, and thus did not seem to threaten any side in the religious, philosophical and political conflicts of the day. As in the case of Witherspoon, McCosh was a much broader person than his sponsors ever dreamed. He brought with him an extensive knowledge of Old World scholarship, not only in Scotland but on the continent as well. In his inaugural address a week after arriving, he proposed to open the door to new disciplines and new knowledge. Andrew Fleming West, who entered as a freshman in 1870 and went on to play a major role as first dean of the graduate school, compared

Engraving of McCosh at age 57. It was done for a campus publication around the time that he assumed the presidency.

Detachable celluloid cuff used as a crib sheet by H.T. Cook, Class of 1871, for one of Dr. Lyman Atwater's logic exams. This was more than two decades before the honor code was adopted.

Student's cartoon of Dr. Atwater, one of the most distinguished members of the faculty for almost 30 years and a favorite target for under-graduate lampooning. He often sharply disagreed with McCosh on matters of policy, and as a conservative theologian was an ardent opponent of the theory of evolution.

McCosh's initial impact to "an electric shock, instantaneous, paralyzing to the opposition, and stimulating to all those who were not paralyzed."

McCosh himself, speaking his characteristic Scottish burr, constantly referred to Princeton as "me college" and delighted in showing visitors its new buildings, saying proudly, "I built that. It's mine." His keen interest in students and faculty would not permit him to pass by anyone on the paths of the tree-lined campus without speaking. Yet at the same time McCosh had a famous inability to remember names. Encountering a bowing student, his greeting was nearly always the same: "I know ye, whooo air ye, whatsyourname?"

McCosh's initial report to the trustees decried the fact that the college library in Nassau Hall was woefully short of books and was open only one hour a week; when he retired it was housed in a building of its own, was open six days a week, contained more than 65,000 volumes, and ranked among the leading college libraries in the United States.

Until his era the long-standing Princeton curriculum allowed few choices. McCosh proposed and established a course of study—modified repeatedly by his successors but still essen-

tially in operation today—under which students take a large number of required courses in broad fields at the start and are permitted elective courses in chosen subjects in later years. He laid down the principle in his inaugural address: "Let the student first be taken...to an eminence, whence he may behold the whole country...lying below him, and then be encouraged to dive down into some special place, seen and selected from the height, that he may linger in it and explore it minutely and thoroughly." William Berryman Scott, a McCosh student in the Class of 1877, wrote with approval that "in Junior year we had for the first time considerable freedom in the choice of our subjects of study. The complete change of atmosphere from the lower class years was most acceptable and I seemed to be entering new and more spacious worlds when I took up physics with Dr. Brackett, psychology with

20th-*century interior view of the reading room at Chancellor Green Library, built in 1873. Below: Marquand Chapel was built in 1881 and destroyed by fire in 1920.*

*P*ortrait of Dr. James Murray, who taught English literature.

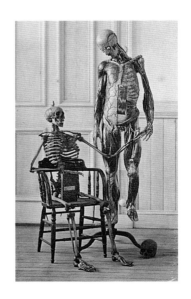

*T*he Manikin and the Skeleton, two notorious 19th-century characters on campus, were longtime companions to Professor John Stillwell "Bones" Schanck, who taught chemistry, zoology, anatomy and physiology for more than 40 years.

Dr. McCosh, logic with Dr. Atwater, geology with Dr. Guyot and, above all, English literature with Dr. Murray. This latter subject was a revelation to me.... I was not content merely to hear and read about the great writers; so far as my very busy life permitted, I read their works, which, of course, made the lectures doubly interesting."

McCosh introduced electives at Princeton at a time when change was sweeping American education in the aftermath of the Civil War. The nation was expanding westward, and its intellectual and scientific horizons, along with its expectations for its colleges and universities, were broadening rapidly. Following an idea pioneered in Germany, universities were increasingly seen as places not only for the transmission of knowledge and values but also for the generation of new ideas for society's benefit, and they were dramatically expanding their scope to include industrial and agricultural arts and professional education in a variety of fields. These developments laid the basis for the creation of great state universities and land-grant colleges following the Morrill Acts of 1862 and 1890; the establishment of such private universities as Chicago, the Massachusetts Institute of Technology, Stanford and Johns Hopkins; and the evolution of Princeton and a number of other previously established American schools into great research universities, with graduate schools as well as undergraduate programs.

At a meeting of the Nineteenth Century Club in New York in 1885, McCosh engaged in a famous debate on the ideal curriculum with President Charles W. Eliot of Harvard, which had eliminated all but a few requirements for undergraduates, leaving nearly every course choice up to the student. In this debate, which became the focus of a national educational controversy, McCosh was on comfortable middle ground as an innovator within a framework of established tradition. While advocating a growing array of choices, he ridiculed a complete freedom "which tempts young men in their caprice to choose easy subjects" or narrow specialities that ignore large bodies of knowledge that have been built up over time. In a famous peroration, which drew heavily on his European experience, McCosh declared: "Tell it not in Berlin or Oxford that the once most illustrious university in America no longer requires its graduates to

Class of 1870 ribbon, the earliest extant use of orange and black.

Class of 1885's 10th-reunion picture on the steps of Nassau Hall. Reunions were well established by the end of the McCosh era.

Arnold Guyot

Dr. Arnold Guyot (right) began the first systematic instruction in geology at Princeton in 1855 and founded Nassau Hall's museum of natural history a year later. Guyot's early work supported the theory of glaciation, and his later work helped establish the field of weather forecasting. Guyot had three mountains, a glacier and a crater on the moon named after him, and the great flat-topped seamounts that characterize many parts of the ocean floor are called "guyots" in his honor. Guyot supported McCosh in his acceptance of Darwin's theory of evolution. Controversy over this theory was still raging in academic circles when this early dinosaur painting by Benjamin Waterhouse Hawkins, titled "Cretaceous Life in New Jersey," was commissioned by Guyot for the Nassau Hall museum.

know the most perfect language, the grandest literature, the most elevated thinking of all antiquity. Tell it not in Paris, tell it not in Cambridge in England, tell it not in Dublin, that Cambridge in America does not make mathematics obligatory on its students. Let not Edinburgh and Scotland and the Puritans in England know that a student may pass through the once Puritan college of America without having taken a single class of philosophy or lesson in religion."

Religion continued to be a central force on the Princeton campus. The Class of 1871, one of the first in the McCosh era, included 21 students preparing for the ministry out of a graduating class of 74 students. In addition, six more class members ultimately entered the ministry. McCosh was a devout Christian who required Princeton students to attend chapel daily and take biblical instruction Sunday afternoons, yet he was broad-minded enough to write on retiring from office, "I have had under me Catholics as well as Protestants of all denominations, Jews and heathen. I have religiously guarded the sacred rights of conscience. I have never insisted on anyone attending a religious service to which he conscientiously objected."

McCosh's most daring stand—and one that caused friction with important leaders of Princeton's highly conservative board of trustees—was his acceptance of the fiercely controversial theory of evolution, which had been denounced on the Princeton campus prior to his arrival. McCosh had written on scientific subjects in Europe and had a deep respect for science; he stoutly maintained that it need not necessarily conflict with religion. In one of his many talks on the subject at Princeton and around the United States, he warned defenders of religion to be cautious in assailing the theory of evolution. "No scientific man under 30 years of age in any country denies it, to my knowledge. To oppose it is to injure young men. I am at the head of a college where to declare against it would perplex my best students. They would ask me which to give up, science or the Bible."

Above all McCosh was a man of ideas. In recruiting a growing faculty he reached out for those who had undertaken advanced study at the best European and American universities

The first Princeton Scientific Expedition went west in 1877, led by Professors Cyrus Brackett and Joseph Kargé. This photograph was taken at Twin Lakes, Colorado. While in Colorado the group encountered a prospector named Stevens who tried to persuade them to invest in his mining. They declined. Stevens went on to establish the famed Iron Silver Mining Company in Leadville, Colorado, which realized millions of dollars in silver ore.

The room of L. Rodman Wanamaker, Class of 1886, at 12 East Witherspoon Hall. Witherspoon was the grandest dormitory in the country when it opened in 1877. McCosh resented the charge that Princeton was becoming a rich man's college, but he admitted that the proportion of wealthy students had increased. Part of his plan to ameliorate this trend was to build Edwards Hall, a much more modest residence than Witherspoon, to house students of limited means.

and, later, tapped young homegrown scholars who had been among the beneficiaries of a broad Princeton education under his own tutelage. Determined to stimulate as well as to instruct, McCosh sought professors whose qualifications went well beyond academic achievement alone. He often asked about a prospective professor, "But mon, is he alive?"

After being at Princeton for a decade, McCosh moved the presidential residence from the President's House near Nassau Hall to Prospect, which had been presented to the college by two philanthropists. There McCosh initiated his famous "library meetings," gathering the best undergraduates, almost all of the graduate students and the most active scholars among the faculty for regular discussions. About half the sessions explored controversial subjects in philosophy and psychology, which were

McCosh's favorites and the subjects he taught. (Today many of these topics would be considered social science, a term unknown in McCosh's day.) Other subjects discussed at the library meetings included the latest scientific discoveries and theories. Biographer J. David Hoeveler, Jr., wrote that the library sessions "demonstrated McCosh's academic commitment to an open atmosphere of learning at Princeton."

An inquisitive and outgoing man, McCosh from first to last was personally concerned about students and student life and was an enthusiast for athletics. In his inaugural address in 1868 he declared that "every college should have a gymnasium for the body as well as for the mind," prompting loud cheers from the students in the audience. Princeton's first gymnasium, a barnlike structure, had burned down three years before.

On November 6, 1869, teams from Princeton and Rutgers met in New Brunswick to play the first-ever intercollegiate football game. With 25 men on a side and no throwing or running with the ball permitted, the game bore more resemblance to later-day soccer than the popular American sport that eventually developed. According to a *Daily Princetonian* history, the game originated in a proposal from William S. Gummere of the

*J*ohn Degnan, circa 1892. "Johnny, Johnny Degnan, do you want me?" was a familiar nighttime taunt shouted from campus dormitories.

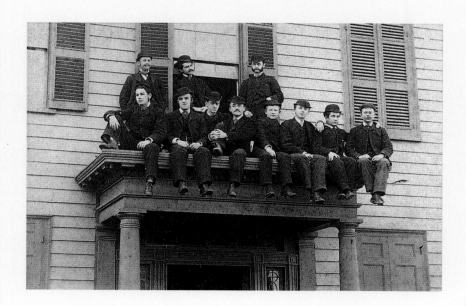

*T*he Brackett Hall gang, a short-lived early eating club in operation around 1880. The members are posed on the porch roof of their clubhouse behind the present Garden Theatre on Vandeventer Street.

Grand Base Ball Match.
COLUMBIA UNIVERSITY
vs.
Nassau Hall.
Admit the Bearer,
TICKETS 20 CENTS.

Class of 1870, later chief justice of the New Jersey Supreme Court, to play ball in place of the annual brawl over a Revolutionary War cannon claimed by both schools. The historic game was played without uniforms, coaches or official scorers. The Rutgers *Targum,* which is the source of the fullest account of the game, reported that Princeton's first goal was made "by a well-directed kick, from a gentleman whose name we don't know, but who did the best kicking on the Princeton side." In the end Rutgers triumphed, six goals to four, as an American tradition was established. Princeton won a return match several weeks later.

McCosh waged total war on Greek letter fraternities and secret societies then prevalent on the campus, and he succeeded after a long struggle in eliminating them. Due to the lack of sufficient dining facilities, however, he tolerated the creation of informal eating groups beyond the campus and gave

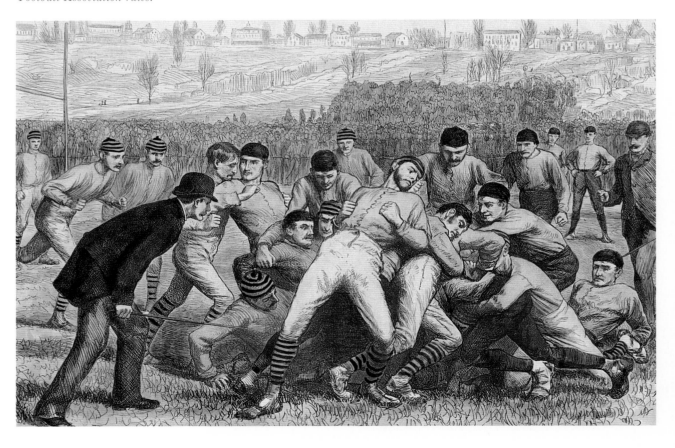

permission for the chartering of Ivy Club, which built a permanent headquarters on Prospect Avenue. Thus began the club system, which has been a source of tension with the administration ever since.

Concerned about student morality, McCosh complained to the trustees that students were gambling, drinking and sneaking away from time to time to Trenton, which he called "the graveyard of purity." On one occasion he resolved, unsuccessfully, to ban student travel to New York after hearing that Princeton football players and student fans had been invited to a special theater performance in their honor, including actresses wearing orange and black outfits, and later participated in an evening of prostitution. He was particularly outraged that this night on the town caused the students to miss church the next morning.

Even more popular than Jimmy McCosh was his wife, Isabella. The daughter of a noted Scottish physician, she discovered on arriving at Princeton that the college had no organized medical service and ordered that any student who was ill should immediately be reported to her. Armed with the list, she made regular rounds of the campus dormitories bearing a basket of

Princeton crew at a regatta in Saratoga, 1875. Crew flourished briefly under McCosh, but was abandoned in 1884 when barge traffic on the Delaware and Raritan canal proved too dangerous for practice or races. The sport resumed after the building of Lake Carnegie in 1906.

George Goldie, perhaps the greatest gymnast of his day, was director of the gymnasium from 1870 to 1911. At age 75 he performed a giant swing on the high bar, then handed in his resignation.

fresh linens, homemade jams, cookies and pots of tea. A student in the Class of 1879 recalled, "She would tap on the door and say, 'May I come in?' But without waiting for a reply she would enter and, after expressing a mother's sympathy, immediately proceed to wash the face, chest and hands of the young man, put the clean sheet on his bed, the pillow case on his pillow, brush his hair and make him as comfortable as possible and encourage him to eat the good things she had brought and to drink a cup of her good tea. Then, sitting down at his desk, she would write a note to his mother, telling her she need not worry about her boy, as 'we are looking after him here.'" Following her husband's retirement, the trustees raised funds for an infirmary building and named it for Isabella McCosh. A successor building, erected in 1925, continues to bear her name.

Starting with his inaugural address, President McCosh often referred to Princeton as a university, though its official name was still the College of New Jersey. In the 1870s McCosh created fellowships for graduate study and established systematic programs leading to master's and doctoral degrees, thereby creating the groundwork for the development of a graduate school, which was an essential step toward achieving true university status. In July 1885, with enrollment temporarily declining, campus disorders rising and alumni support sagging, McCosh formally

Isabella McCosh

SHE WAS EVEN MORE POPULAR THAN JIMMY McCOSH

Isabella McCosh (opposite), from an oil painting by John White Alexander, Class of 1881, presented as a gift from the artist just before her death at age 92. Daughter of the eminent Scottish physician Alexander Guthrie, she possessed a keen intellect and an aptitude for medicine. Her skills were extremely important not only on campus, but also in the town of Princeton, which as yet had no hospital. Andrew Fleming West, Class of 1874 and later Princeton's first dean of the graduate school, was one of the legion of students who benefited from Isabella's care. He commented upon her long and capacious life that "its circumference was the outmost bound of the circle of persons she could benefit."

The original Isabella McCosh Infirmary, built in 1892-93.

1888 *photograph showing the corner of East College, Nassau Hall with the skylit museum in back, the old chapel and the dead Bulletin Elm, a landmark tree that had been part of Princeton life since its planting by Samuel Stanhope Smith during the Witherspoon era. It got its name from all the broadsides and bulletins posted around the trunk, making it the campus information center for nearly a century.*

C*yanotype (opposite) of McCosh in retirement, at his home on Prospect Avenue.*

S*till-green leaf from the Bulletin Elm found pressed in the scrapbook of C.B. Bostwick, Class of 1896.*

proposed to change the institution's name to Princeton University as a way to rekindle enthusiasm. The highly conservative trustees, who had become increasingly critical of McCosh's progressive ideas, voted the proposal down, leaving this symbolic step to his successor.

In November 1887, after nearly 20 years as president, McCosh resigned, confident that Princeton was a university in all but name and headed for greater things. "So I retire," he declared in his farewell message. "The college has been brought to the very borders [of a university], and I leave it to another to carry it over to the land of promise."

He and Isabella moved out of Prospect to a house on the site of the current Quadrangle Club. He continued to teach philosophy to an undergraduate class and selected graduate students. His tall, stooped figure could frequently be seen in daily walks around the campus with his distinctive derby hat and cane. The pathway on the campus leading to Washington Road and Prospect Avenue, one of his favorite spots for strolling, was named McCosh Walk in his honor. Early in the 20th century McCosh Hall, the site of many lecture and seminar rooms, was built and named in his memory.

Following his retirement, the members of the Class of 1889 unanimously asked that their diplomas bear his signature along with that of his successor, Francis L. Patton. McCosh was moved to tears at the request from the student delegation from "me college" that called on him with their request. When he died on November 16, 1894, students rang the bell at Nassau Hall to spread the news and mourn this beloved figure. His death came 100 years and one day after that of his fellow Scotsman and Princeton predecessor, John Witherspoon.

Grand aisle of elms! your graceful arms,
your trunks grown dark from storm,
Your canopy o'erhead
Cathedral arches form.
Your shaded cloisters echo praise,
As soft the branches sway,
Of the grand old man who daily walks
Beneath your vaulted way.

EDWARD J. PATTERSON, CLASS OF 1894

McCosh on McCosh
Walk. Engraving in Scribner's
Magazine *of 1897.*

The Graduate School

IN ADDITION TO EDUCATING STUDENTS, THE
GRADUATE SCHOOL HELPS ATTRACT FACULTY
WHO ARE LEADERS IN THEIR FIELDS.

Andrew Fleming West
(center), first dean of the graduate
school, shares a joke with Thomas
Edison at the commencement
of 1915. General George W.
Goethals, builder of the Panama
Canal, walks at West's left. West
served as dean for 27 years.

Formally established in 1900, the graduate school's origins date back almost to Princeton's beginnings. While records are spotty, the first resident graduate student seems to have been a Scottish native, Daniel Thane of the Class of 1748, who stayed on after receiving his A.B. degree to study theology under President Burr even before the College of New Jersey had moved to Princeton. James Madison of the Class of 1771, who stayed on for six months' study under the tutelage of President Witherspoon, may have been the first Princetonian to pursue

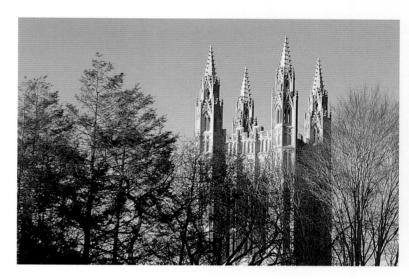

nontheological postgraduate study. The number of graduate students increased to nearly two dozen in the early 1800s, but their work was informal and they were not granted advanced degrees.

The 173-foot Cleveland Tower was erected by public subscription as a memorial to Grover Cleveland, President of the United States and chairman for many years of the trustees' committee on the graduate school.

President McCosh brought from Scotland the ideas that laid the foundation for a school of graduate study. He spoke in his inaugural address of the need for "higher scholarship" and special fellowships and vigorously pursued the goal of a graduate school modeled on that at the University of Edinburgh. By the time of his retirement in 1888, 78 graduate students were enrolled in courses of study ranging from art to physics. The first graduate course in engineering was offered in 1889.

It was not until 1901, five years after Princeton officially became a university, that the graduate school opened for business. The trustees appointed as the founding dean Andrew Fleming West, Class of 1874, who did more to shape the school's development than any other person. Dean West, who established a high standard of academic excellence, is best known for his bitter struggle with President Wilson over the location of the Graduate College, as the residential facilities of the school came to be known.

In the end West prevailed, and the imposing collegiate Gothic halls of the Graduate College were built across the golf course, remote from the rest of the campus.

Through the years since, the graduate school has grown and diversified. Unlike many other institutions, Princeton has maintained a single faculty that conducts research and instructs graduate students as well as undergraduates, and it has resisted demands for separate professional schools in fields such as law, medicine and business administration.

In the late 1950s President Goheen and the trustees decided to expand the graduate school rapidly in response to a national shortage of college and university faculty members. This decision, which ultimately expanded the number of graduate students nearly threefold to about 1,500 by the end of the 1960s, was a major factor in facilitating the university's acceptance of coeducation in 1969. Because of the growth of the faculty that accompanied the enlargement of the graduate school and the availability of a significant number of graduate student instructors, the undergraduate college could be expanded by the admission of women without a corresponding increase in the size of the faculty. This helped to make the coeducation decision not only highly desirable but surprisingly affordable.

The graduate school itself admitted its first female student in 1961 under rules that permitted entrance only to women who qualified for studies that were unavailable elsewhere. The graduate school became fully coeducational with the rest of the university in the late 1960s. In the 1994-95 academic year, 37 percent of the 1,790 graduate degree candidates

were women, 33 percent were citizens of other countries, and 13.2 percent were American students from minority groups. Graduate students were enrolled in 37 departments and programs, in most cases working for the Ph.D., except in the School of Architecture and the Woodrow Wilson School of Public and International Affairs, where the typical terminal degree is a master's. Alumni of the graduate school account for almost 25 percent of the Princeton alumni body.

A large number of outstanding scholars have attended Princeton's graduate school, including every Princeton president since John Grier Hibben, Class of 1882, the immediate successor to Woodrow Wilson. In addition to educating students, the graduate school also makes a critical contribution to the overall quality of Princeton by helping to attract faculty who are leaders in their fields. Many of Princeton's most beloved and distinguished teachers of undergraduates would not be at Princeton if they did not have the opportunity to teach graduate students as well.

1916 *pen and ink sketch of the garden at Wyman House, built next to the Graduate College in 1913. Below: Oil portrait of Beatrix Jones Farrand, who came to Princeton in 1912 at age 30 to design the landscape for the new Graduate College. Over the next 31 years she transformed much of the main campus as well.*

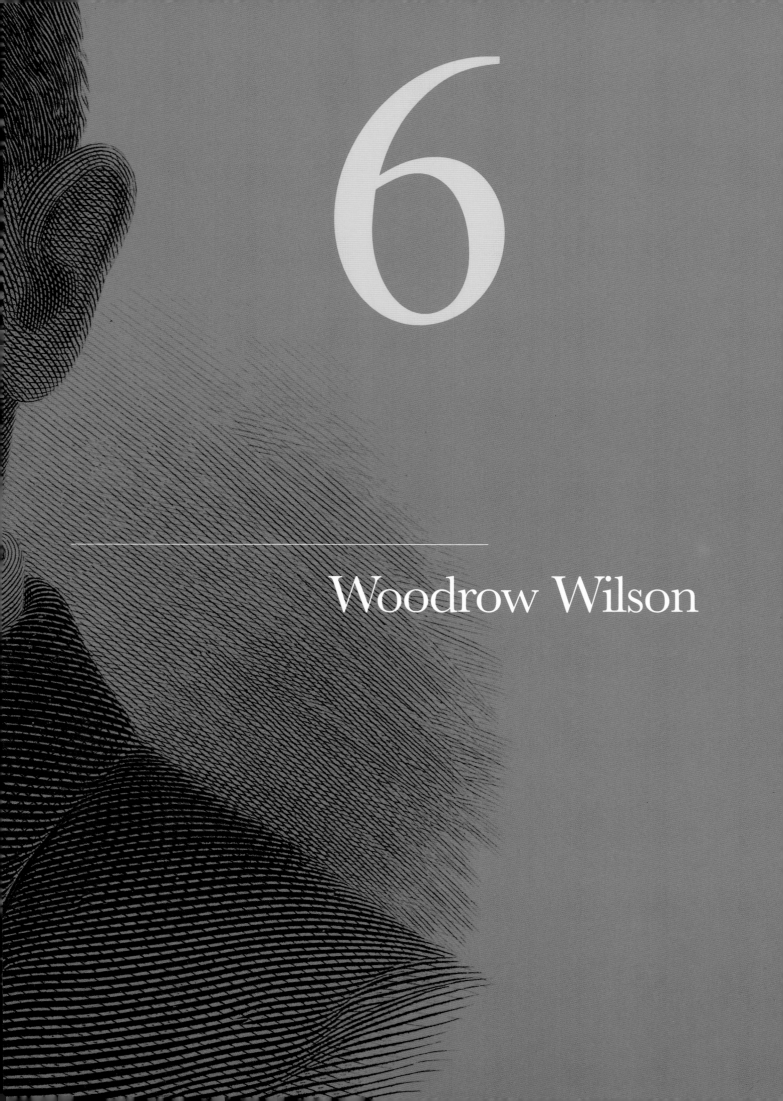

6

Woodrow Wilson

Woodrow Wilson, the 13th president of Princeton and 28th President of the United States, was the most influential—and most controversial—Princeton figure of the 20th century.

A graduate of Princeton and a highly popular professor, Wilson launched an unparalleled tide of educational reform after becoming Princeton's president in 1902. Following extensive change in the curriculum, in 1905 he introduced the preceptorial system, beginning a tradition of active student participation in the learning process that has been a central feature of Princeton's educational method ever since. With that single act he increased the size of the faculty by 50 percent. These distinguished young preceptors built Princeton's academic strength and helped transform a burgeoning residential college into a leading research university.

Flush with success but shaken by a sudden physical setback (in retrospect, probably a stroke that prefigured the ones years later that disabled him amid his White House battle for the League of Nations), Wilson then proposed a sweeping reform of undergraduate life and fought an uphill battle over the location and autonomy of the Graduate College. When he lost both battles in the face of powerful opposition, Wilson abruptly left Princeton to accept the Democratic nomination for Governor of New Jersey in 1910. Two years later the meteoric Governor Wilson won the U.S. presidency.

"McCosh cleared the ground and laid the foundation for the university," wrote Professor Joseph R. Strayer '25 in a 1953 report on Princeton's academic development. "Wilson completed the structure and gave it a form which has not been greatly changed by any subsequent additions." Professor Arthur S. Link, a Wilson biographer and editor of the 69-volume Wilson Papers project, wrote that "Wilson had a larger hand in the development of Princeton into a great university than any other man in the 20th century. He left a vision of an institution dedicated both to things of the mind and the nation's service, promoted a spirit of religious tolerance and held up the ideals of integrity and achievement that still inspire the Princeton community."

W*ilson as president of Princeton, striding across campus in cap and gown.*

Thomas Woodrow Wilson, who was known as Tommy to his classmates but who dropped his first name later in life, was the oldest son of an Ohio printer who became a Presbyterian minister and served various churches in the South. Wilson arrived at Princeton as an undergraduate in September 1875 when President McCosh was revitalizing the college. His freshman year was grueling, but as a sophomore he found himself and embarked on what he later called "the magical years." He was introduced to great political tracts, such as the Federalist Papers

President Grover Cleveland reviewing a mile-long torch-light procession during Princeton's sesquicentennial celebration. Over 2,000 people participated in the moonlit October 21, 1896, march, which was an unforgettable sight to all who witnessed it. Nassau Hall glowed with orange electric lights. The campus was adorned with Chinese lanterns and both orange and black bunting and the stars and stripes. The evening's finale came in a burst of fireworks.

and histories of England, formed his own debating club and became managing editor (and later editor) of the *Princetonian.* "Wilson's second year at college was among the most important of his whole life: a turning point," wrote Ray Stannard Baker, an early biographer. As a senior he made "a solemn covenant" with his closest classmate to "school all our powers and passions for the work of establishing the principles we held in common; that we would acquire knowledge that we might have power."

After law school at the University of Virginia and a frustrating effort to establish himself as an attorney in Atlanta, Wilson obtained his Ph.D. at Johns Hopkins and embarked on a fast-track academic career that took him to Bryn Mawr and Wesleyan before he was summoned to Princeton in 1890 by President Patton, who had succeeded McCosh two years earlier.

Handsome and articulate, Wilson quickly became the most popular professor on campus. In 1896 he delivered his famous sesquicentennial address on "Princeton in the Nation's Service" at the ceremonies in Alexander Hall. "When all is said and done," he declared, "it is not learning but the spirit of service that will give a college place in the public annals of the nation. It is indispensable, it seems to me, if it is to do its right service, that the air of affairs should be admitted to all its classrooms.... There is laid upon us the compulsion of national life. We dare not keep aloof and closet ourselves while a nation comes to its maturity."

*W*ilson as a Princeton student, Class of 1879.

*P*resident Francis Landey Patton reading his newspaper on the porch at Prospect.

WARNING!

WHEREAS,

WE, THE MEMBERS OF THE GALLANT, GREAT AND GLORIOUS

CLASS of '90
OF
PRINCETON COLLEGE,

the undisputed lords of all creation, and the masters, owners and trainers of those filthy, foul and fiendish brutes and reptiles which constitute that menagerie which is commonly known as the

FRESHMAN CLASS
OR THE CLASS OF '91,

have transported the above accursed animals from the lowest depths of Hades to this earthly paradise of ours, in the hope that thus coming in contact with GENTLEMEN and SCHOLARS they might possibly lose some of their beastly traits and become in some small degree civilized; and

WHEREAS,

We have been deeply disappointed and greatly grieved to perceive their base ingratitude and disgraceful conduct, "SCARCELY PARALLELED IN THE MOST BARBAROUS AGES,"

THEREFORE,

We have deemed it fitting and proper to give this PUBLIC WARNING to the inhabitants of Princeton and vicinity to beware of the actions of these vicious creatures; although we shall do our utmost to protect the public from their depredations by keeping them closely confined behind the bars of their cages.

WE ESPECIALLY PROHIBIT their carrying any description of a CANE

at any time or under any circumstances, or degrading those immortal colors, THE ORANGE AND BLACK, by displaying any scrap of them upon their persons or within their filthy dens. After MATURE DELIBERATION we have decided to give a

Daily Exhibition

of these wonderful phenomena in the Gym. from 12 to 1.   The chief attractions are as follows:

First comes the two-fold reptile whose color is symbolical of the character of the whole tribe, the 'GREEN' tomato 'WORM[S],' otherwise known as the 'VERDENT' 'Lion.' A 'LEACH' next comes upon the stage, but is quickly swallowed up by a 'POOR' 'ROBIN[S],' who then perches on a 'STUMP' and makes 'BETTS' on how the deuce to pronounce MUSEGH MINASSIAN.
It gives us pleasure to announce next the patriarch MOSES, who will appear in his great role of 'ADONIS.' The famous 'TROTTER' Maud S. will then be led from her 'BARN[ES]' and driven around the track while 'SPUANS' gives a SPICY exhibition of vomiting.
At the close of the performance 'YOUNG' Freshman HERRICH will render 'HOME, SWEET HOME' in his own disgusting way while the man in the 'ATHLETIC DEPART-MENT' scans the advertisements in the back of Owen's Homer.
FRESH cigarettes furnished between the acts by MURRY, the would-be life preserver.

ADMISSION FREE!
FOR GENTLEMEN ONLY.

Like many of his contemporaries on the faculty, Wilson was increasingly disenchanted with the leadership of Patton, who was described by one professor, in a memorable phrase, as "a wonderfully poor administrator." In confidential maneuvers that only became public many years later with the publication of the Wilson Papers, Wilson helped persuade influential trustees that Patton should be ousted for the good of the university. Patton was willing to go quietly but at a price that equaled his salary for six years. The money was secretly raised by trustees and benefactors. Upon Patton's resignation, Wilson was immediately and unanimously elected Princeton's president. He was the first layman, following a long line of clergymen, to be named to the post.

Broadside (opposite) posted by the sophomore Class of 1890. Above: The snowball massacre of 1892. Three freshmen in the Class of 1895 (l-r: Darwin James, John Poe and Arthur Wheeler) suffered serious injuries from a well-aimed sophomore fusillade.

Arguably the century's most ridiculous student riot occurred in May 1899 when a mob of Princeton students attacked Pawnee Bill's Wild West Show as it paraded down Nassau Street. The infamous melee that resulted received widespread coverage in the national press. Such collegiate peccadilloes had become a staple for the readers of both racy tabloids and the more conservative news periodicals. As reported in the New York Sun: "Suddenly a rock came out of the throng, striking a cowboy named Big Mouth on the wrist. When Big Mouth retaliated by lashing several students with a whip, the mob began bombarding the wagons with cannon crackers and old eggs. This caused a stampede down the street until Pawnee Bill rallied his forces and charged the students. Numbers were against him, however, and in the end Indians, cowboys, and wagons were in full flight."

Habitual neglect of class work was followed by hasty cramming for final exams, which often solely determined a student's grade. The cramming was interrupted each night at 9:00 p.m. sharp when the din of horns, drums, tin pans and firecrackers, the flight of flaming tennis balls and the report of pistols signalled a short break called "Poler's Recess." Poler was an early epithet for one who was thought to study too zealously. This ritual started before the turn of the century and lasted, sporadically, until the 1950s. This recess photo was taken in 34 University Hall in 1915.

Although Princeton had grown extensively during Patton's 14-year administration, doubling its enrollment from 600 to more than 1,300 students, formally establishing a graduate school and officially becoming a university, its educational quality had not kept pace. Classes were large and conducted almost entirely through lectures and examinations. While dozens of new subjects had been added to the curriculum, this had been done in an uncoordinated and haphazard way. It was easy to be admitted to Princeton and almost impossible to flunk out. Under Patton, according to Moses Taylor Pyne, a member of the Class of 1877 and one of the most influential Princeton trustees, "study was not dignified, nor was it absolutely essential." Wilson, when asked early in his presidency how many students there were at Princeton, answered "about 10 percent."

One important innovation during the Patton regime, in which Wilson played a part, was the establishment in 1893 of the honor system. This took place at the instigation of students who were upset with the amount of cheating on examinations. The students, including two from Tennessee who had attended a prep school that relied on an honor code, took their concerns to Wilson's wife, Ellen, who brought her husband into the discussions. Wilson took the lead in convincing the faculty to approve the honor system, describing it then and later as entirely a student initiative. Under the honor code students explicitly agree not to cheat on examinations, exams are not proctored, and a student committee deals with reported violations. Subsequently adopted by many other colleges, it remains a vital part of Princeton academic life and tradition.

Five years before becoming president, Wilson had outlined to his brother-in-law, Stockton Axson, the three big things he would do if he were given the power: "First, he would reform the curriculum; second, he would reform the method of teaching; and third, he would reform the plan of college life." That is precisely what Wilson sought to do, with brilliant success on the first two fronts and abject failure on the third.

Wilson's reform of the curriculum arose from extensive discussions within the faculty that predated his presidency but were ignored by his predecessor. Under his plan juniors and seniors were permitted increasingly to specialize in departments of their own choice, even though freshman and sophomore years remained heavily weighted with required subjects. High-ranking seniors were also permitted to substitute independently prepared

*M*athematics instructor Charles "Bull" Hinton devoted himself to developing a theory on the fourth dimension of space and inventing a baseball pitching machine that could change speeds and throw curves. The ball was propelled from the machine's cannon-like muzzle by a powerful gunpowder charge. It scared batters half to death and quickly fell into disuse.

*P*rinceton Banjo Club group portrait, circa 1911.

papers of their choosing for one course. This was the start of Princeton's emphasis on undergraduate independent work and a forerunner of the eventual requirement of the senior thesis, which became the most distinctive feature of a Princeton education. Wilson observed in his annual report to the trustees in 1904 that "the movement of courses the four years through is from general to special" but that "at no point is there opportunity for narrow specialization and at no point a chance to disperse the attention over a miscellany of unrelated subjects." Variations of Wilson's plan were subsequently adopted by Harvard, Yale and other colleges. It has continued to be the principle governing later revisions of the Princeton curriculum.

The town is small, the college large. It is properly secluded, but not remote; and it gives a chance for the rearing of ideals upon equal support of the active and contemplative life. Friendliness between colleagues and by the help of preceptorial teaching in small groups, between student and teacher...does much to effect in students just what a university ought—to teach them the art of living a good life.

CHARLES G. OSGOOD, PROFESSOR, 1905

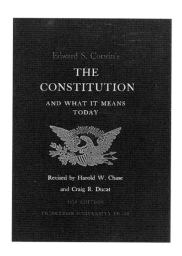

Edward Corwin had just completed his doctorate in history and was jobless when he applied for one of Wilson's preceptorships in 1905. He eventually held the McCormick Professorship of Jurisprudence, a chair first occupied by Wilson himself. Below: After 14 editions, Corwin's The Constitution and What It Means Today, first published in 1920, is still in print.

Christian Gauss (opposite, top), one of Wilson's 50 original preceptors, stayed at Princeton for 41 years, becoming probably the best-known dean in America. Literary mentor to F. Scott Fitzgerald '17 and Edmund Wilson '16, he had more than 40 books dedicated to him by former students. In retirement, Gauss, a diehard football fan, glumly watches the Tigers lose at Palmer Stadium. Charles Grosvenor Osgood (opposite, bottom), known as "the dean of Princeton humanists," traveled to New York twice a week for workouts at a gym with Babe Ruth.

Wilson's most famous academic reform, the preceptorial system, was modeled on the English tutorial system. In an address to New York alumni within weeks of his inauguration, Wilson announced his intention to pioneer "radical change in our conception of an education." He called for replacing lectures and textbooks in the upperclass years with small group meetings and independent study led by young but accomplished scholars, who would be "companions and coaches and guides." He told the alumni, "Gentlemen, if we could get a body of such tutors at Princeton we could transform the place from a place where there are youngsters doing tasks to a place where there are men doing thinking, men who are conversing about the things of thought." The object, he said on another occasion, was "to take our instruction as much as possible out of the formal classrooms and get it into the lives of the undergraduates, depending less on lectures and written tests and more on personal conference and intimate counsel."

Wilson asked the trustees to authorize the hiring of 50 preceptors, or tutors, at an annual salary of between $1,500 and $2,000 each. The total faculty at that time was only 109. Together with other changes he proposed, Wilson's list of immediate and pressing needs came to a staggering $6 million at a time when the university's total annual expenditures were only $456,000 and its

Oswald Veblen, another original preceptor, was the first occupant of the Henry Burchard Fine Professorship, the first American research chair in mathematics. He relinquished this position in 1932 to become the first professor at the new Institute for Advanced Study (pictured under a rainbow). In addition to his own pioneering work in geometry, relativity theory, symbolic logic and topology, he helped relocate many scientists from Nazi-dominated Europe to the institute. An avid outdoorsman, he donated his forested 81-acre Princeton home, Herrontown Wood, for use as a park.

total endowment only $3.1 million. The trustees may have gasped, but they allowed Wilson to proceed as finances permitted. Wilson raised enough money and pledges from alumni to launch the preceptorial system and began a whirlwind course of personal recruitment.

Crucial to the enterprise, Wilson recognized, was the ability to inspire as well as to instruct; therefore, teaching skills as well as scholastic qualifications were vital. Wilson scoured the country for young scholars, declaring they should not be kept in the demanding jobs he had in mind for more than five years. By June 1905, 47 of the planned 50 preceptors had been chosen and given the rank of assistant professor. Others were added later. Undergraduates accepted the innovation with curiosity and enthusiasm, as recorded in a new verse of the Faculty Song:

> *Here's to those preceptor guys,*
> *Fifty stiffs to make us wise.*

It was certain almost from the first that the preceptorial system would not meet Wilson's sky-high expectations for it. In general the preceptors kept closer to the texts and lectures than Wilson suggested they would. A few of them proved to be inspiring teachers; many others were simply very competent purveyors of academic knowledge in small group meetings.

Neither Wilson nor his successors were very clear about how the famed system was to work in practice. The faculty minutes for the year it was introduced contain only one administrative reference to the far-reaching innovation, and no official statement or description appeared in the university catalog until four years later. Over the years Wilson's high expectations for the preceptorial system have been fulfilled in some instances and disappointed in others. Many Princetonians recall precepts as among their most valuable educational experiences, while others have been less impressed, including a departing senior quoted in the *Alumni Weekly* as saying, "The preceptorials were like sex, highly overrated."

Whatever its long-term value, the immediate impact of the introduction of the preceptorial was to make Princeton overnight the most exciting university in the country for young scholars. Wilson chose his preceptors personally and wisely. Edward G. Conklin, who was recruited to be a professor of biology, later wrote that "a professor from another university, who had come to Princeton about the same time that I did, said to me, 'What brought you to Princeton?' I answered, 'Woodrow Wilson. And you?' 'The same,' he said. Both of us were inspired by his ideals of a university, of education, of life, and we wanted to join with him in the great work he was doing." Many of Princeton's most illustrious professors, and many who went on to the top ranks of other schools, were recruited by Wilson in his initial drive. When the last of the Wilson preceptors retired in 1946, Princeton counted among them four deans, nine heads of departments and one trustee. It is not too much to say the preceptors proved to be the foundation of Princeton's academic greatness in the first half of the 20th century. Despite Wilson's initial intention that preceptors remain for only five years, 21 of the original 50 remained on the Princeton faculty until retirement.

The pathos of the situation [is] that I cannot impart to you from my experience anything that will keep you from being just as great a fool as I was at your age.

WILSON SPEAKING TO HIGH SCHOOL STUDENTS, 1908

GO AS FAR AS YOU LIKE

R.F. Outcault

Postcard of Princeton trampling an opponent by Richard Felton Outcault, who created a hugely successful newspaper cartoon called "The Yellow Kid." The mass popularity of this garishly hued comic gave rise to the pejorative term "yellow journalism."

Princeton's first intercollegiate basketball team, formed in 1901-02, had a record of 7-5. The University Gymnasium, built in 1903, provided an excellent new facility for the infant sport, invented just 12 years before. Photo is of Samuel S. Schmidt '19.

By the spring of 1906 Wilson was at the height of his popularity at Princeton. A trustee referred to him, in a much-repeated phrase, as "Princeton's most valuable asset." But at just this moment he awoke in late May to blindness in his left eye. Specialists in Philadelphia diagnosed the trouble as a burst blood vessel and blood clot that was a symptom of hypertension, although later studies suggested it was also a stroke. Wilson canceled his schedule for the rest of the semester, including his appearance at commencement, and went to England for three months' rest. He seemed to recover rapidly, although the sight in his left eye was never fully restored.

When he returned in the fall, Wilson plunged into new enterprises and controversies in a way that surprised some of his close friends. Outwardly as self-confident as ever, he seemed now to be a man in an even greater hurry. He obtained tentative approval of his "quad plan" to abolish the Prospect Avenue eating clubs and reorganize the campus into self-sufficient quadrangles by vote of the trustees without consulting the faculty, alumni or students, a defect that contributed to the plan's rejection. His failure to pave the way was surprising, since he himself acknowledged in his initial proposal that this sweeping change in undergraduate life was "heretical in character," especially as it meant an all-out battle with the clubs, by then firmly established as the social focus of the upperclass years.

Wilson was among the first, but by no means the last, to charge the clubs with undermining the "old democratic spirit" of Princeton. Nor was he the last to be confronted by opposition to change on the part of prominent alumni enthusiasts of club life and the social connections that flowed therefrom. Following the furor that erupted as soon as the plan was published in mid-1907, the trustees judged it to be unworkable. With the underlying tensions unresolved, the university's relationship with Prospect Avenue continued to be complex and uncomfortable long after the Wilson era. In the 1980s, some three-quarters of a century after it was proposed, a modified version of Wilson's quad plan—a system of "residential colleges" for all freshmen and sophomores—was finally instituted at Princeton.

More personal and ultimately even more destructive for Wilson than the struggle over the quad plan was his losing battle with Dean Andrew Fleming West over the permanent location of the Graduate College. Wilson demanded that graduate students

Ceremonial groundbreaking shovel used by Wilson to initiate construction on 1879 Hall.

Undergraduate "Tommy" Wilson (holding his hat) posed with other members at his eating club, the Alligators.

RECEPTION AND SMOKER
IN HONOR OF
WOODROW WILSON, '79
GIVEN BY THE
PRINCETON ALUMNI ASSOCIATION
OF THE DISTRICT OF COLUMBIA
THE NEW WILLARD   MARCH 3, 1913

*S ongbook for an inaugura-
tion reception for Wilson on
March 3, 1913, given by the
Washington, D.C., alumni
association.*

*W ilson (opposite) with
French President Raymond
Poincaré in 1918 upon his
arrival in Paris. Below:
Wilson's portrait on the
$100,000 bill. Only one series
of these bills was ever issued,
in 1934; they never circulated
to the general public, but were
used solely to transfer funds
between the Treasury and the
Federal Reserve.*

live and work in the midst of the revitalized undergraduate life, while West insisted on a more remote site across the golf course, where graduate students could be cloistered in a life of their own. Wilson, already weakened by the opposition to his quad plan, was defeated when West obtained several large contributions to underwrite construction of the Graduate College on a site that he preferred, where it remains located today. The decisive contribution came from the will of a West devotee who suddenly died and left an estate designated for West's plan. The estate was estimated at the time to be worth $3 million, although in the end it proved to be much less. "We've beaten the living," Wilson told his wife, "but we can't fight the dead."

Having been thwarted twice in high-profile battles, Wilson was at the end of his Princeton career. With influential trustees maneuvering for his removal, Wilson bowed to the entreaties of several prominent political managers that he accept the Democratic nomination for Governor of New Jersey. He resigned the presidency of Princeton in the fall of 1910. Leaving behind a university that had been both fundamentally reformed and beset by controversy during his administration, Wilson embarked on a political life in Trenton that quickly served as a stepping-stone to the White House.

Princeton in the Nation's Service

Woodrow Wilson's sesquicentennial address of 1896, "Princeton in the Nation's Service," proclaimed a commitment that had characterized the university since its founding and provided a motto that Princetonians have rallied around ever since. In 1956, during the centennial year of Wilson's birth, an anonymous donor established a prize to honor Wilson and recognize exemplary service to the nation. The award is presented annually on Alumni Day to an alumnus or alumna of the undergraduate college for service in fields that have ranged from government, education and foreign affairs to religion, philanthropy, medicine, journalism, science, public advocacy and the arts. In his 1994 commencement address, President Shapiro asked whether the time had come to broaden Wilson's phrase to encompass service to other nations. "In the world that lies ahead of us," he said, "serving our nation and serving the world must—in some respects—be one and the same."

Winners of the Woodrow Wilson Award, 1956–1995

Norman Armour '09
Allen O. Whipple '04
Charles L. House '09
Bayard Dodge '09
Raymond B. Fosdick '05
Clinton T. Wood '21
Adlai E. Stevenson '22
Henry deW. Smyth '18
Nicholas deB. Katzenbach '43
William F. Ballard '27
Eugene C. Blake '28
Harlan Cleveland '38
Walsh McDermott '30
John B. Oakes '34
George P. Shultz '42
Ralph Nader '55
John D. Rockefeller III '29
Claiborne deB. Pell '40
John M. Doar '44
George F. Kennan '25
Thomas P. F. Hoving '53
Henry R. Labouisse, Jr. '26
Robert F. Goheen '40
Paul A. Volcker, Jr. '49
Lewis Thomas '33
John A. McPhee '53
James A. Baker III '52
William D. Ruckelshaus '55
Donald H. Rumsfeld '54
William H. Hudnut III '54
William W. Bradley '65
Frank C. Carlucci '52
T. Berry Brazelton '40
James M. Stewart '32
Laurance S. Rockefeller '32
James H. Billington '50
Wendy S. Kopp '89
Sidney D. Drell '47
Douglas I. Foy '69

Wendy S. Kopp '89, whose Teach for America program originated in her senior thesis, with her adviser, sociology professor Marvin Bressler.

Adlai E. Stevenson '22, then Governor of Illinois, with Triangle Club performers Craig Nalen '52 and Wells Huff '52, from the 1949-50 production, Come Across. *Stevenson ran for President of the United States in 1952 and 1956 and later served as U.S. ambassador to the United Nations under Presidents Kennedy and Johnson.*

7

The Interwar Years
World War I to World War II

One popular ritual of the early 20th century was the annual flour picture (previous page and below). Sophomores dumped flour and rotten fruit on the freshman class as it posed on the steps of Whig Hall for its first class photograph. This tradition died out by the late 1920s.

Upperclass students at an eating club formal dinner.

When the growing national allure of higher education following World War I provided Princeton for the first time with more applicants than it could admit, it adopted a policy of selective admission in 1922. As applied, the policy led to a notable narrowing of the makeup of the student body and contributed to Princeton's reputation as a country club for the socially elite, which later proved difficult to shake.

At the same time, Princeton was advancing impressively in terms of academic quality. In 1923 the Upperclass Plan of Study, popularly known as the Four-Course Plan, was inaugurated, leading by the end of the decade to the adoption by nearly all departments of the senior thesis as the required capstone of independent research. It quickly became a hallmark of a Princeton undergraduate education.

In 1930 the School of Public and International Affairs, later named the Woodrow Wilson School, was established to bring history, politics, economics and other disciplines to bear on the issues of the nation and the world. Interdepartmental programs in the humanities and the arts followed.

The most dramatic developments, however, came not in humanistic Princeton but in scientific Princeton. With the assistance of Rockefeller Foundation funds, Princeton became a haven for a number of European scientists taking refuge from Adolph Hitler. Adding to the luster of an already distinguished scientific faculty were figures such as Eugene Wigner, who later won the Nobel prize in physics, and John von Neumann, author of *Theory of Games and Economic Behavior* and an intellectual father of the computer. The presence of Albert

Einstein, one of the great scientific figures of all time, at the Institute for Advanced Study, which was first housed on the campus and then in nearby buildings of its own, made Princeton the most renowned center in the world for physics and mathematics.

❧

The end of World War I in 1918 set off what seemed an avalanche of applications for admission. "America had come of age during the war, and one sign of maturity was the conviction that more education for the entire population was desirable and possible," wrote Professor Joseph Strayer in his 1953 report on Princeton's academic development. Nassau Hall responded to the intensified interest in higher education by easing some outdated requirements; for example, Greek was dropped as a requirement for the A.B. degree in 1919 (although Latin was still required). Applications soared. A prewar freshman class of over

THE TIGER

MASCULINE NUMBER

Tiger with monocle, from the November 1920 issue of Tiger Magazine.

In 1921 Dean Henry Burchard Fine went to New York to pick up Albert Einstein (left), who had chosen Princeton for a lecture series on his new theory of relativity. Scientists from all over the United States packed McCosh 50 for the five talks. Einstein moved to Princeton 12 years later.

ROTC bayonet drill on the south campus during World War I.

Gas Masks.

German Masks

Masks
German French

Pictures from an ROTC training album showing the different types of gas masks in use in the trenches of Europe. The photographs were taken atop Holder Tower. Below: Trenches at south end of campus.

400 was considered phenomenal, but freshman classes after the war jumped from 424 in 1919 to 631 in 1922—more than the university felt it could house, feed and educate.

The trustees established the principle of selective admission in 1922 when they placed a cap on the undergraduate body of about 2,000 students. The entering freshman class was limited to about 600, and Radcliffe Heermance, an assistant professor of English, was named the first full-time director of admission. This imposing, strong-minded administrator filled this post for a generation. As he prepared to retire in 1950, the *Nassau Sovereign*, an undergraduate magazine, said with only slight exaggeration that "the Princeton of the last 25 years has probably been influenced more by Dean Radcliffe Heermance than by any other single person or factor."

Before the war Princeton had established special relationships with a number of preparatory schools in order to guarantee itself a steady flow of qualified freshmen. Now these relationships came into full flower. By the mid-1930s a confidential report to the committee on admission revealed that "Princeton is unique among all American institutions for higher education in drawing five-sixths of its entering group from private preparatory schools and only one-sixth from public high schools." Looking back at the interwar years, a later director of admission, C. William Edwards '36, reported that the number of applicants to Princeton decreased rather steadily in the 1930s as "high school boys were staying away from Princeton in droves." He added, "There was growing concern that the decreasing application list represented a narrowing geographically, economically, socially and academically."

There were no black students at Princeton in the 1920s and 1930s. President John Grier Hibben told University of Chicago President Robert M. Hutchins that "they just don't seem to want to come"; in fact, Princeton discouraged them from doing so. The number of Jewish students, which had never been high, dwindled to fewer than 20 per class after the first year of

Uniformed members of the Class of 1918 singing "Old Nassau" at their commencement ceremony. Half the class was already in active service, and the normally colorful pennants of such an occasion were replaced by ominous stacks of guns. Professor, now Colonel, William Libbey, Class of 1877, led the procession, followed by President Hibben and Secretary of State Robert Lansing. Libbey, on active duty at the time as a rifle instructor for the Army, was 63 years old when the United States entered the war.

selective admission and never exceeded that number until World War II. When challenged later, Heermance stoutly denied there had been a quota. However, research in the 1970s by Marcia Graham Synnott produced extensive evidence that the number

Triangle Club

The Princeton College
Dramatic Association presented
its first performance, David
Garrick, in 1883. Garrick
started two traditions that survive
to the present day: a national
tour and men dressing as women.
In 1893 the association changed
its name to Triangle Club. The
club's first production, The
Honorable Julius Caesar, was
written by Booth Tarkington
1893. Reviewing one of the early
shows, Professor Stockton Axson
wrote: "What these players lack
in technique, they make up for by
their superior intelligence and
manifest glee in acting." Triangle
erected its first home, the Casino,
on the lower campus in 1895.
It also served as a dance hall,
tennis court, bowling alley, and
armory for the National Guard.
The Casino burned down in
1924, and by 1930 the club
had a new home at McCarter
Theatre. Clockwise from upper
left are "girls" from Zuider
Zee, 1928-29; Tabasco Land,
1905-06; Once over Lightly,
1938-39; The Mummy
Monarch, 1906-07; The Man
from Earth, 1922-23; and
What a Relief, 1935-36.

of Jews was kept deliberately low. "I hope the Alumni will tip us off to any Hebrew candidate," wrote V. Lansing Collins, Class of 1892, the secretary of the university and a member of the committee on admission, in a 1922 letter dug up by Synnott. "As a matter of fact, however, our strongest barrier is our club system."

Since Wilson had lost his battle for the quad plan, the club system had increasingly come to dominate upperclass life. Three-fourths of the upperclassmen were club members in the 1920s, and nine-tenths were members in the 1930s. The comfortable and sometimes elaborate facilities, the professional waiters in white coats and grand party weekends created an aura of elitism in the jazz age for which Princeton became widely known. "Horde of Girls Due Here This Weekend" was the headline on the front-page story in the *Daily Princetonian* of May 2, 1929, listing by name and hometown each of the 700 female guests descending on Prospect Avenue for that year's houseparties weekend.

F. Scott Fitzgerald '17, who popularized the university's image as an academic sandpile for the rich, called it "the pleasantest country club in America." Fitzgerald's 1920 novel, *This Side of Paradise*, which catapulted him to fame at age 23, waxed poetic about Princeton's social landscape as seen by an immature undergraduate: "Its lazy beauty, its half-grasped significance, the wild moonlight revel of the rushes, the handsome, prosperous big-game crowds, and under it all the air of struggle that pervaded his class."

F. *Scott Fitzgerald '17 (top), billed as the "most beautiful showgirl in the Princeton Triangle Club's new musical play," also wrote the lyrics for* The Evil Eye, *1915-16. The dust jacket cover from the first edition of* This Side of Paradise *is from Fitzgerald's personal scrapbook.*

Literary critic Edmund Wilson '16 added to the image by writing in 1923, "At Princeton, too great seriousness tends to be considered bad form or merely unnecessary...[the students] walk back and forth to their meals at large eating clubs which look rather like country clubs, while gold canopies of autumn leaves pave the sidewalks where they lounge." Novelist and social critic Upton Sinclair wrote caustically in 1926 that "Princeton is the first school of snobbishness in the United States."

Paradoxically, Princeton was rapidly developing physically and academically while it was acquiring a playground reputation. Under Hibben, the conciliator and consolidator who followed the dynamic Wilson as president from 1912 to 1932, undergraduate enrollment increased from 1,391 to 2,298, with a further increase in the graduate school. Meanwhile, full-time faculty increased from 166 to 287, the budget tripled, and the endowment more than quadrupled. The area of the campus doubled from 62 acres to 120 acres, giving rise to an impressive array of dormitories, classrooms, laboratories and other facilities, including the University Chapel and Palmer Stadium. Referring to the building boom, Professor Charles G. Osgood wrote, "Never in all her history was Princeton the scene of such Aladdin magic as unfolded itself during the last 12 years of the Hibben administration."

The New Plan of Study, adopted in 1923, was the major educational advance of the period. Conceived by Luther P. Eisenhart, a renowned mathematician and one of the university's most inspiring teachers, it built on the principles of McCosh and Wilson of increasing flexibility and concentration on a chosen field in the junior and senior years. Virtually an honors program for the entire upperclass student body, it was popularly called the

Edmund "Bunny" Wilson '16, from a cartoon in the New York Review of Books and as an undergraduate.

Four-Course Plan because it substituted independent work for one of the customary five courses taken by juniors and seniors. The New Plan led within a few years to the requirement in almost all departments of a senior thesis. The thesis quickly became a distinctive centerpiece of a Princeton education, so much so that over 40 percent of alumni polled by the university in 1973 named it "the single most valuable academic experience at Princeton." Nothing else came close.

The Great Depression that followed the Wall Street crash of 1929 left its mark on Princeton. Each year scores of students were forced to withdraw for financial reasons. So many parents

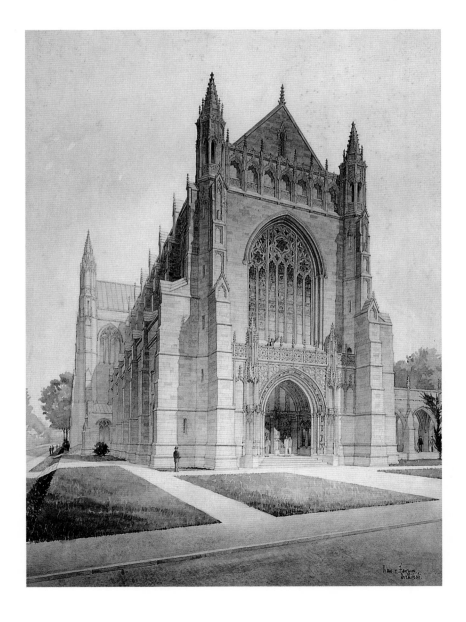

*O*n houseparties weekend, *1920, a suspicious fire destroyed the old Dickinson Hall and beautiful Marquand Chapel. Students in tuxedos joined with firefighters in trying to douse the flames. The firm of Cram and Ferguson, which had previously designed the Graduate College, won the contract for a new chapel (left), built primarily of Indiana limestone, that was completed in 1928.*

*F*ootball team of 1932 practicing on University Field, the site of today's Engineering Quadrangle. When Palmer Stadium was built in 1914, games were shifted to that much larger and grander venue.

1935
commencement issue of Tiger Magazine.

and students defaulted on their fees that the university adopted a rule requiring everyone to pay tuition in advance before registering for courses. In the "bank holiday" of 1933, banks throughout the nation were closed down temporarily by the government, leading the *Daily Princetonian* to issue scrip for use at retail stores, movie theaters and barber shops in town. "The *Princetonian* intends to show its confidence in the banks and in the checks of undergraduates," the paper declared solemnly.

On another front, the 1930s brought a surge in Princeton's reputation in physics, building on a tradition going back a century to 1832, when Joseph Henry was named professor of natural philosophy. Henry, who later went to Washington as the first secretary of the Smithsonian Institution, was the greatest—some say the only—research physicist of his time in the United States. He rigged wires on campus to experiment with physical principles of electromagnetic induction, which became the basis for the telegraph. Henry's distinguished teaching and research in the sciences was continued by a number of later mathematicians, physicists and other scientists, especially between 1903 and 1928 under the sponsorship of Henry Burchard Fine, who served as chairman of the Mathematics department, dean of the faculty and dean of science.

The rise to power of the Nazi party in Germany in the 1930s created an uncomfortable and eventually untenable climate for many European intellectuals and scholars. Princeton, aided by a special scientific fund of the Rockefeller Foundation, did some world-class recruiting. Eugene Wigner, a Hungarian who later won the Nobel prize for physics for his nuclear theories, recalled that he was an assistant professor at the Institute of Technology in Berlin in 1930 when he received a cable from Princeton offering a visiting professorship at about eight times his existing salary. "I thought this was an error in transmission. John von Neumann received the same cable, so we decided that maybe it was true, and we accepted." In the months to come many other top European scientists joined them.

When the Institute for Advanced Study was founded in 1930 to provide a congenial home for the exploration of "pure science and high scholarship" on the part of great scientists, it was initially housed in the original Fine Hall, the mathematics building on campus, before moving at the end of the decade to its own quarters a few blocks away. (The original Fine Hall was renamed Jones Hall when the Mathematics department moved to the new Fine Hall in 1970.) While the institute was never organizationally part of Princeton University, its very close academic and intellectual ties have made it a major asset to the university.

Princeton got too tough for me, so I transferred to Harvard.

JOHN F. KENNEDY '39, 1960

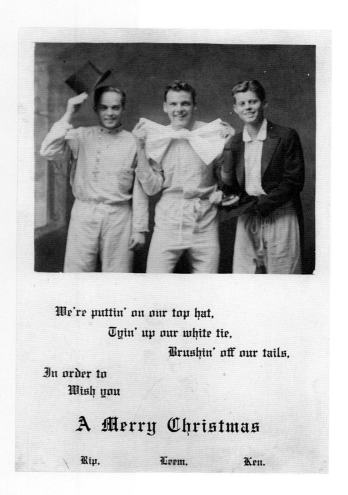

We're puttin' on our top hat,
Tyin' up our white tie,
Brushin' off our tails,
In order to
Wish you

A Merry Christmas

Rip.   Leem.   Ken.

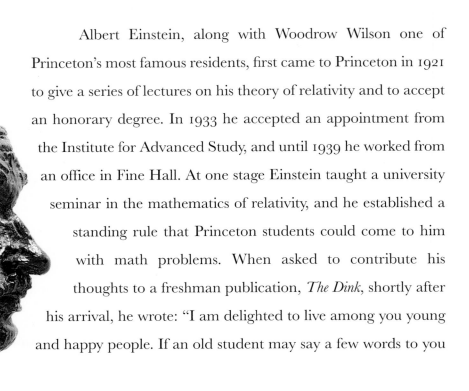

Albert Einstein, along with Woodrow Wilson one of Princeton's most famous residents, first came to Princeton in 1921 to give a series of lectures on his theory of relativity and to accept an honorary degree. In 1933 he accepted an appointment from the Institute for Advanced Study, and until 1939 he worked from an office in Fine Hall. At one stage Einstein taught a university seminar in the mathematics of relativity, and he established a standing rule that Princeton students could come to him with math problems. When asked to contribute his thoughts to a freshman publication, *The Dink*, shortly after his arrival, he wrote: "I am delighted to live among you young and happy people. If an old student may say a few words to you

Cunning is the Lord God, But malicious He is not.

*A*lbert Einstein walking at the Institute for Advanced Study. When Princeton awarded Einstein an honorary degree in 1921, Dean Andrew Fleming West saluted him as "the new Columbus of science, voyaging through strange seas of thought alone." Jacob Epstein's bust of Einstein is in the Fine Hall library.

they would be these: Never regard your study as a duty, but as the enviable opportunity to learn to know the liberating influence of beauty in the realm of the spirit for your own personal joy and to the profit of the community to which your later work belongs." Even after moving to the new buildings of the institute, Einstein continued to live a stone's throw from the Princeton campus at 112 Mercer Street and often took part in university activities.

The combination of the university's outstanding Mathematics and Physics departments and the presence on campus of Einstein and the institute made Princeton in the 1930s the world center of theoretical physics. As World War II approached in 1939, Einstein wrote a letter to President Franklin D. Roosevelt that paved the way for the development of the U.S. atomic bomb. Many Princeton scientists played key roles in the wartime Manhattan Project, which produced the first U.S. nuclear weapons.

Meanwhile, in the depths of the depression in 1933, Harold W. Dodds *14, professor of politics and chairman of the newly established School of Public and International Affairs, succeeded Hibben as Princeton's president. "We are in the midst of a revolution which does not appear to be of our own seeking; our objectives are confused, our attack uncertain," Dodds told students and faculty in the opening exercises of his first year. Nevertheless, he continued, "the prospects of high adventure in living are more alluring today than ever. We are in a mood to experiment. In this lies the strength and hope of the present generation."

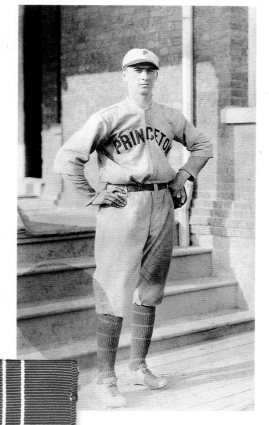

Moe Berg '23, arguably the greatest baseball player ever to don the orange and black, played in the major leagues for 15 years, even though it was said that "he could speak a dozen languages and couldn't hit in any of them." A colorful but mysterious figure, he became one of America's top spies; his espionage work in Nazi-occupied Europe won him the Presidential Medal of Freedom (now at the Baseball Hall of Fame).

Colonel Victor I. Morrison '05 swearing his son, Victor, Jr., '45 into active service with the Marines in 1942. Opposite: Lieutenant Jimmy Stewart '32 of the Army Air Corps, who saw intense aerial combat over Germany as pilot of a B-24 Liberator bomber.

The fourth naval vessel to carry the name U.S.S. Princeton was a 10,000-ton aircraft carrier, christened by Mrs. Harold Dodds in 1942. It was destroyed by Japanese aircraft in the Second Battle of the Philippine Sea, October 1944.

Dodds was faced with the challenges of the depression, followed by preparations for war, which was visible on the horizon by the end of the 1930s. "No matter what the future holds," Dodds declared at the June 1940 commencement, which was held the day after Italy declared war on an already beaten France, "the university pledges its full cooperation with our government in its program of national defense...." Within days he created a university Committee on National Defense and instructed it to make a detailed inventory of what individual faculty members and academic departments could contribute to a war effort. Consequently, much planning had been done when Japan attacked Pearl Harbor on December 7, 1941. Two days later, following the U.S. declaration of war on Japan and Germany, Dodds sent the following telegram to Washington:

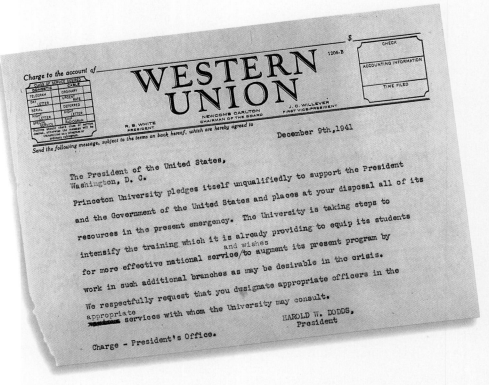

WESTERN UNION

December 9th, 1941

The President of the United States,
Washington, D. C.

Princeton University pledges itself unqualifiedly to support the President and the Government of the United States and places at your disposal all of its resources in the present emergency. The University is taking steps to intensify the training which it is already providing to equip its students for more effective national service/to augment its present program by work in such additional branches as may be desirable in the crisis. and wishes

We respectfully request that you designate appropriate officers in the appropriate ~~xxxxxxx~~ services with whom the University may consult.

HAROLD W. DODDS,
President

Charge - President's Office.

World War II and its aftermath, as Dodds may have foreseen, would bring the most rapid and extensive changes in Princeton's history.

THIS WEEK
MAGAZINE
NEW YORK
Herald Tribune
(Copyright, 1942, New York Tribune, Inc.)

MAY 17 1942

SECTION X

★ ★ ★ ★ ★ ★ ★ ★ ★ ★ ★ ★ ★ ★ ★ ★ ★ ★

In this Issue

STAR. This is Lieutenant James
Stewart, U. S. Army Air Corps.
The Lieutenant was one of Holly-
wood's brightest stars until
March, 1941. He was drafted,
trained as an Aviation Cadet, became an officer. Jimmy is just
one of the many movie headliners
in uniform now. For others, see
"Sidelines," Page 2.

Harold W. Dodds, 1933-57

"IT WAS A SURPRISE TO ME, AND QUITE A SHOCK," HE SAID LATER. "THE LAST THING IN THE WORLD I WANTED TO BE WAS A UNIVERSITY PRESIDENT. BUT I FELT I EITHER HAD TO ACCEPT THE OFFER OR LEAVE TOWN."

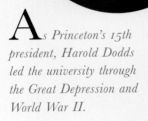

A*s Princeton's 15th president, Harold Dodds led the university through the Great Depression and World War II.*

Born: Utica, Pennsylvania, 1889. B.A., Grove City College, Pennsylvania, 1909. M.A., Princeton, 1914. Ph.D. in Politics, University of Pennsylvania, 1917. Died: Hightstown, New Jersey, 1980.

Harold Dodds was professor of politics and chairman of the newly created School of Public and International Affairs (now the Woodrow Wilson School) when he was selected to be Princeton's 15th president in 1933. "It was a surprise to me, and quite a shock," he said later. "The last thing in the world I wanted to be was a university president. But I felt I either had to accept the offer or leave town."

Dodds took office in the depths of the Great Depression and guided Princeton through World War II and the Korean war. He presided over the bicentennial celebration in 1946-47. During his tenure the student body (including graduate students) increased from 2,600 to nearly 3,600, and the size of the faculty nearly doubled. The new buildings erected in the post-World War II portion of his tenure included Firestone Library and Dillon Gym. The Annual Giving program began during his presidency, in 1940.

Bidding farewell to the graduating class at the 1957 commencement, his last as president, he declared: "My fondest wish for every member of the class is that each one of you will have an experience similar to mine; that you will find a work which you love above everything else under circumstances which spell fulfillment; and that you may have the good fortune to find it in a place which you love above all other places on earth."

Dodds *in his presidential robes (above) and hamming it up for the camera. Princeton grew in size and stature during his tenure, significantly expanded its commitment to graduate education and research, and became increasingly diverse.*

8

Post-World War II Princeton

The gaily dressed crowd of 5,000 guests on the front lawn of Nassau Hall sat beneath ancient elms on the bright sunny day of June 17, 1947, as Princeton celebrated the end of its bicentennial year and, without being fully conscious of it, the beginning of an era that would bring the greatest changes in all its history.

Marching through the FitzRandolph Gate to their places on or just below the Nassau Hall platform were members of the black-gowned procession of nearly a thousand celebrants, including representatives of 43 other nations. Leading the way were President Dodds and U.S. President Harry S Truman, the only two speakers at this climactic moment of the bicentennial celebration.

"Princeton enters her third century with certain convictions as to what she wants her future to be," Dodds declared in his address from the Nassau Hall platform. "We shall uphold the banner of the general as the only safe foundation for the particular. We shall strive for quality rather than quantity; we have no illusions of grandeur that bigness will satisfy."

World War II had brought shifts in thinking and emphasis that would change Princeton in the years ahead. The results of the war placed the United States in a greater position of international leadership and responsibility than ever before in its history. The victory had been won in

Princeton religion scholar dies at 89

PRINCETON TOWNSHIP — Horton Marlais Davies, an authority on the history of Christianity who taught at Princeton University for almost 30 years, died Wednesday at his home here. He was 89.

A member of the Princeton faculty from 1956 until 1984, he wrote more than 30 books, including "Worship and Theology in England," a five-volume work published by Princeton University Press in the 1960s and 1970s.

A native of South Wales, Davies earned his bachelor's and master's degrees at the University of Edinburgh and his doctorate in philosophy from Oxford.

He joined the faculty at Rhodes University, South Africa, in 1947, and

"His teaching interests ranged widely through arts and literature while his scholarship centered in the history of worship and religious practice," said John Wilson, the Agate Brown and George Collord Professor of Religion Emeritus. "Generations of undergraduates and graduate students, as well as his colleagues, treasured his insights and his wit."

In 1993, his autobiography, "A Church Historian's Odyssey: A Memoir," was published. He also co-wrote "Sacred Art in a Secular Century" with his son Hugh.

"My father loved Princeton deeply as it was both his home and his profession for 50 years," Hugh Davies said.

"He was enormously proud of the university's high standards and of the caliber of the faculty and students. I would often tease him by saying he must be jealous that he wasn't an alum himself, and he would just smile."

Davies is survived by his wife, Marie-Helene Davies of Princeton; a daughter, Christine Pisani of Tarrytown, N.Y.; two sons, Hugh Davies of La Jolla, Calif., and Philip Davies of Gloucester, Mass.; five grandchildren; and his first wife, Brenda Davies of Newtown, Pa.

A memorial service will be held at 2 p.m. Thursday at Trinity Church, 33 Mercer St, Princeton.

ceive a
gation.
quity

quity

President Cras
than 30 people applied for
sition.

Bauer, principal at the Charles
W. Lewis Middle School in
Gloucester Township since 1996,
will be paid $110,000 to take the
top spot in the district. She has a
doctorate of education from
Rowan University and a master's degree in educational ad-

"We ended up with five
really good candidates," h
"What finally decided us w
enthusiasm. I think sh
grow with this district a
be a good fit. I think s

Robber pleads guilt

By LINDA STEIN
Staff Writer

TRENTON — A city man serving a 20-year prison term for rob-
bing two taxi cab drivers
pleaded guilty yesterday to tam-
pering with a witness.

ie" Singleton,
d at a halfway
Luther King
his arrest, was
in 2003 of rob-
in September
released from
s before those
erving nearly
bing cab driv-

ers in Newark, Assistant
cutor Randolph Norris sa

Singleton admitted tha
to his trial he sent two th
ing letters to a witness,
his saliva used to seal t
lopes, Norris said.

"I addressed corres
to her asking that this
resolved," Singleton to
rior Court Judge Bill M

"You asked her to a
instead of going to cou

Although the letters w
via a third party, Single
linked to them by the
the other in Spanish, re
that she not testify agai

Colon. One was in Eng
ing letters to a witness,

large part because of the superior scientific and technical prowess of the United States, organized under government auspices. The struggle against forces of bigotry and racism fostered a stronger belief in religious and racial equality, in time extending to equality for women, than had been the case before. All these developments would have an impact as Princeton entered its third century.

❦

In the period immediately following the end of the war, the university made special arrangements to receive the veterans whose Princeton years had been interrupted, reinterviewing and readmitting more than 2,000 former students who had left for the war or who had been admitted during the war but had been unable to attend because of military service. Because of this surge of returning veterans, augmented by other veterans now being admitted for the first time, the campus in 1946 was crowded with more than 3,400 undergraduates, more than could be permanently accommodated and far beyond its prewar peak of about 2,400 students. Cots were installed in Baker Rink; Brown Hall was turned over to married veterans; and commencements were held three or four times a year as returning students completed their requirements under an accelerated course of study.

*M*arried students in 1946 moving onto campus (above) and sharing kitchen facilities at 19 University Place, another overcrowded married housing facility. "This generation is used to having no privacy," said one returning war veteran.

As the bulge of veterans receded, the demand for higher education did not. Nationally about 15 percent of the college-age population had attended colleges or universities before the war, but by 1950 this had doubled to 30 percent. This was largely due to the G.I. Bill of Rights, which made college an affordable possibility to all who served in the armed forces, and to national prosperity and an increasing realization that a good education was the pathway to a good job. Despite the rising demand for admission, Dodds, in keeping with his bicentennial vow to keep Princeton relatively small, drew the line at about 2,800 undergraduates and about 500 graduate students.

Under Dodds' guidance, the faculty once again made revisions in the undergraduate plan of study. This time each department was encouraged to develop a broad introductory course for underclassmen, and all entering students were required to take at least one course in each of four general areas: mathematics and the natural sciences; the social sciences; the humanities; and the generally related areas of history, philosophy and religion. The "distribution requirements," as they were called, aimed to give each student an overall acquaintance with the major fields of study and discourage premature specialization. They remained essentially unchanged for half a century until the faculty in 1995 adopted a revised and somewhat broadened set of requirements, effective with the Class of 2000.

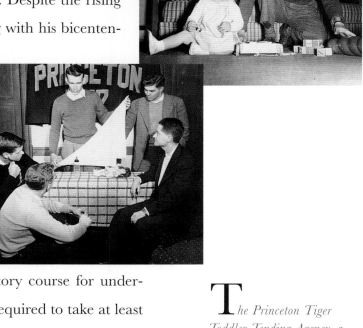

The Princeton Tiger Toddler Tending Agency, a student entrepreneurial venture, capitalized on the sudden postwar baby boom by placing undergraduates in part-time child care jobs.

In September 1948, in the midst of an atmosphere of postwar change and expectation, I got off the Pennsylvania Railroad train from my hometown of Atlanta, Georgia, at Princeton Junction; trudged through the now-familiar tunnel under the tracks lugging a big suitcase, a duffel bag and a heavy coat for the winter ahead; and boarded the Dinky. Coming from a small public high school, it was with awe, mixed with equal parts of fear and enthusiasm, that I began my Princeton career.

The Class of 1952, of which I was a member, was the first post-World War II class that had only a few veterans and therefore was considered the first "normal" Princeton class of the new era. The 801 young men made up the largest freshman class up to that time and had the greatest geographical distribution and the highest proportion of public high school alumni (35 percent) compared to prep school graduates. The class included 54 Jewish students, nearly twice as many as the peak number before the war. In the spirit of the time, the class was considered more democratic and less socially elitist than earlier classes. Even so, there were no black students; there were only a handful of Asian-Americans; and, of course, there were no women.

The campus that my classmates and I inhabited was replete with signs of physical change. The new Firestone Library was opening its doors for the first time. Dillon Gymnasium, which had been built on the site of an earlier gym destroyed in a World War II-era fire, was newly opened and the center of athletic life. Physical education, as programs of regular exercise were called, was required for freshmen. More than three-fourths of us went on to participate in intramural sports, a striking feature of undergraduate life before and since. Today two-thirds of all students still participate in intramural sports, making Princeton extraordinary in the extent of organized physical activity.

It is hard to believe now, but prewar Princeton tradition, which was being revived as we entered, required all freshmen to wear black caps with little bills known as "dinks" until released from that duty by victory over the sophomores in the annual cane spree competition or by some other liberating event. Most of us thought this ridiculous and demeaning and would have

Tiger Magazine cover in 1932 equating the wearing of "dinks" with carrying the weight of the world on one's back.

1947 etching of Dillon Gymnasium. The gym was commissioned in conjunction with the bicentennial celebration.

Chemistry Professor Hubert Alyea '24, presenting one of his famed pyrotechnic lectures. Walt Disney Studios used Alyea's flamboyant personality as the model for their movie character, "The Absent-Minded Professor."

none of it. After a while sophomores finally gave up a vain effort at enforcement. That was the end of the tradition.

Academically, it was a vibrant time. Albert Einstein was living on Mercer Street and was often seen on campus in his baggy sweatshirt and heard in the cause of world government. There were many outstanding and exciting professors, including E.H. (Jinx) Harbison '28 in history, Alpheus T. Mason *23 in jurisprudence, the spectacular Hubert Alyea '24 in chemistry and the most beloved of all, Walter P. (Buzzer) Hall. Buzzer, as he was called because of the noise of his early-vintage hearing aid, was an unorthodox and flamboyant professor of European history, known especially for his passionate portrayal of his hero, the Italian insurgent Garibaldi. When he retired in my senior year, his final lecture had to be moved from McCosh to Alexander Hall, and he was given a seven-foot scroll with the names of undergraduates who had contributed to a special academic fund in his honor.

The defining event of our student era, and one that forged a high degree of class unity and spirit, was our demand that all of us who wished to belong to a Prospect Avenue eating club be given at least one bid, or invitation. In several previous years, a small number of club applicants had been left out, effectively leaving them unable to participate in the central elements of upperclass social life and with little alternative to two more years of the uninspiring fare of the commons dining halls. Arguing that "we members of the sophomore class feel it necessary for us to demand that all men admitted to Princeton be accepted into the social system of the upperclass years as well as the academic life of the university," 610 of us declared in a petition that we would all boycott the clubs unless every classmate who chose to join received at least one bid. Such an act would have

B*lack ball box once used at an eating club during the bicker process. Balls were dropped in secretly, and when the box was opened, the presence of a single black ball would disqualify a candidate.*

W*alter Phelps "Buzzer" Hall came to Princeton in 1913 as a preceptor and stayed for 39 years, becoming one of the most popular professors of all time. His introductory course on modern European history helped make History one of the largest departments at Princeton. "He gave himself freely, and...received in return the affection of his colleagues and of generation after generation of undergraduates," said Professor Joseph Strayer '25, a former student of Hall's who later chaired the department.*

bankrupted a number of the clubs.

It is hard to recapture today the passionate controversy that "the 100 percent petition" touched off. After an intense struggle involving Nassau Hall, the Graduate Interclub Council, upperclass club members and a steering committee

A Holiday Magazine pictorial on Princeton in 1950 depicted the extent to which campus social life revolved around the eating clubs. The student's date and her luggage were picked up at the Dinky station, then she was taken to a club party, kissed goodnight, and housed for the weekend on the club's top floor.

of our class officers, the *Daily Princetonian* announced in huge type on March 9, 1950, after a late-night bargaining meeting, "ALL SOPHS GET BIDS." We had won our struggle, but that was by no means the end of it. The 100 percent goal was achieved, though often with great difficulty, until 1958, when 23 sophomores were left out, 13 of whom were Jewish. This prompted a new controversy and renewed calls for reform.

Meanwhile, as my classmates and I were taking our stand for egalitarian treatment of those already admitted, a drive was underway against the exclusion of minority groups, especially blacks, from admission to Princeton. Up to this point, the university had been essentially lily-white, even though early in its history several black students studied as private students of President Witherspoon, and a free black from Virginia may have been enrolled briefly in 1793. Princeton early in the 20th century discouraged black applicants, telling them, as President Wilson suggested, that it was "altogether inadvisable for a colored man to enter Princeton."

As World War II approached, Princeton's reputation for racial bias drew increasing objections as the nation joined the

fight against prejudice in Nazi Germany. Norman Thomas '05, the perennial Socialist Party candidate for president and a respected gadfly, complained in a 1940 letter to the *Alumni Weekly* that "Princeton maintains a racial intolerance almost worthy of Hitler and wholly alien to any ideal of a university or even a college in a democracy." Two years later the editor and the editorial-page editor of the *Daily Princetonian* trained attention on the issue in a series of controversial and hard-hitting editorials headed "White Supremacy at Princeton." Meanwhile, the U.S. Navy sent four black students to Princeton under its wartime V-12 program. One of them, Arthur Jewell Wilson, Jr., '48, was the basketball team captain in 1945-46. Another V-12 student, John L. Howard '47, became the first of his race to obtain an undergraduate degree at Princeton. But after the war ended black students were a rarity.

The barrier came down after the New Jersey state legislature began passing antidiscrimination legislation in 1947-48.

Norman Thomas

CLASS VALEDICTORIAN AND SIX-TIME SOCIALIST CANDIDATE FOR PRESIDENT

Norman Thomas '05 at his 50th reunion. "None of us at Princeton in 1905 could possibly have dreamed what this half-century has brought forth. But I suspect that in years of war and turmoil, among our comforts has been satisfaction that Princeton and the things it stands for have endured. Often we have warmed our hearts at the flame of our Princeton loyalties. And Princeton's beauty, present before our eyes or in memory, has been like Princeton's friendships, an abiding joy, a part of life's wealth that cannot be taken away."

While Princeton took a stand against this "coercive legislation," saying it would not work, President Dodds officially notified the trustees in June 1949 that the new laws applied to the processing of applicants for admission. That fall three black students were among the incoming freshmen. But Princeton's enrollment of blacks remained minimal, with no more than two black students per class during the 1950s, even while civil rights was among the burning national issues of the day.

University proctors on Blair steps in 1949 (l-r): Harold (Pete) Swasey, John Cuomo, Harry Cauley, Michael Kopliner, Joseph Sweeney and Francis X. Hogarty. The office of the proctor was instituted in 1870 by President McCosh to help him discharge the heavy disciplinary burden that his predecessor, John Maclean, had to handle by himself.

As late as January 1962, Princeton's official position was that, while it did not discriminate against blacks, a special recruiting effort would be unfair to other applicants. This began to change as a result of intensive Nassau Hall discussions involving President Robert F. Goheen '40 and his aides. In October 1962 E. Alden Dunham '53, a newly hired director of admission who had previously worked closely with Harvard President James B. Conant in his studies of public education, told the *Daily Princetonian* he was working to "consciously seek out qualified Negro applicants." The following summer, in his first annual report to President Goheen, Dunham declared that "it is important to increase the number of Negroes at Princeton" in the interest of diversity, which for the first time was defined as embracing race as well as geography. If there are to be larger numbers of blacks at Princeton, Dunham said, "they must be actively recruited," because of the small pool of qualified applicants and Princeton's long Southern tradition.

Heightened awareness of a racial crisis in the country greatly affected sentiment on the campus and decisions in Nassau

Arthur Jewell (Pete) Wilson, Jr., '48 (left) and James Everett Ward '48 entered Princeton as members of the Navy's wartime V-12 program. Wilson became captain of the basketball team.

Martin Luther King, Jr., with Assistant Dean of the Chapel Carl Reimers and chapel deacons on the steps of Chancellor Green in 1960. When Dean of the Chapel Ernest Gordon, who had been corresponding with the civil rights leader for several years, invited King to deliver the Sunday sermon, the invitation was widely criticized. King spoke again at Princeton in 1962.

Hall. A precipitating factor was the October 1963 appearance on campus of Governor Ross Barnett of Mississippi, an outspoken advocate of racial segregation, at the invitation of Whig-Clio at a time when students and the nation at large were caught up in the drama of integration in the South. Barnett's speech prompted a widespread protest from undergraduates, graduate students, faculty and the Princeton community.

On October 13 Goheen made a dramatic appearance before a capacity crowd of 1,200 in the now-defunct Playhouse movie theater, which had been taken over for the evening by the Princeton Association for Human Rights. "The Revolution of 1963," as Goheen and others called it, "is both a real social force and a long-deferred claim for fair and fruitful opportunities, which every American must recognize," he declared. The president called on the entire community—town and gown alike—to work toward the achievement of "equal and open opportunities in all areas" for blacks. He announced that the university real estate office would no longer list any rental property where there was evidence of discrimination and that discussions had begun with the university's building contractors about their employment practices. In admissions, he declared, "we are making concerted efforts to attract more Negro applicants into the university."

Eleven days after his speech, Goheen raised the issue with the board of trustees. Quoting from what he had said publicly, Goheen said it was difficult for him to disassociate his own convictions from the conduct of his office, and that it seemed "necessary and right" that the trustees should know just where he stood on this issue and "how strongly" he felt about it. While saying that he did not propose to reform the whole nation or tell Southern communities what to do, he declared that the univer-

Carl Fields

Jerome Davis '71

When Carl A. Fields arrived at Princeton in August 1964 as assistant director of student aid he was the first black administrator at any predominantly white university in the nation. Princeton had only 12 black students at the time, but many more would be arriving in future years. Fields anticipated the problems these pioneers would face and played an essential role in helping them and the university make a successful adjustment. Fields initiated the Family Sponsor Program, through which the local black community provided social and emotional support; helped to establish the nationally influential Association of Black Collegians; and conceived the Frederick Douglass Award, given annually on Class Day to a graduating senior who has "contributed unselfishly towards a deeper understanding of the experience of racial minorities." Fields went on to become assistant dean of the college and chair of the university's human relations committee. He saw a black student (Jerome Davis '71) serve as president of the Undergraduate Assembly, and he helped create the Third World Center in 1971, his final year at Princeton. Right: On Class Day 1968, Dean of Students William D'O. Lippincott '41 presented the first Frederick Douglass Awards to seniors Paul Williams (left) and Deane Buchanan.

sity must address itself to the critical problem of upgrading educational opportunities for young blacks, specifically helping more of them to qualify for Princeton admission. The university cannot take a pose of "disengaged concern" about the issue but must "reach out a helping hand and try to do so in a genuinely effective manner," the president said.

After a general discussion of the issue, Harold H. Helm '20, a native Kentuckian who was chairman of the trustees' executive committee, approved Goheen's statement and said it was clearly Princeton's duty "as a great institution" to do everything it could.

The decision to recruit blacks actively was a fundamental turning point. A nationwide drive was then launched, and the number of black undergraduates on campus began to climb, from seven in 1962 to 41 in 1966 and 318 in 1970. The number of black students in the first-year class leveled off in the 1970s to between 80 and 100 most years, despite active efforts by the admission office and alumni schools committees to attract more blacks to Princeton. Nonetheless, it was no longer true that, as the *Daily Princetonian* had said in the mid-1960s, the black in the university's colors "refers to tiger stripes—and not to people."

Commenting in 1977 on the celebrated Bakke case, in which a white student charged the medical school of the University of California at Davis with reverse discrimination, President William G. Bowen *58 defended Princeton's practice of refusing to set quotas but taking race into account along with other factors in admission. The Bowen standard, along with a similar policy at Harvard, was cited by Justice Lewis Powell in his swing-vote U.S. Supreme Court opinion banning quotas but upholding special consideration for disadvantaged groups.

In a speech at opening exercises in 1982, Bowen said that Princeton since the mid-1970s had entered a period of "consoli-

Members of all groups appear to feel that there are too few "safe" spaces within the university in which discussions about race can take place...without accusations, hostility and recriminations.

VICE PROVOST
RUTH SIMMONS

R*uth Simmons served Princeton as the first director of studies in Butler College, acting director of the Afro-American Studies program at a pivotal time in its history, assistant and associate dean of the faculty, and vice provost before being elected president of Smith College in 1995. In 1993 she was the author of a landmark report on race relations at Princeton.*

A *widely shared commencement sentiment.*

dation" with regard to the admission of minority students, a time of greater stability with modest increases in overall numbers. While diversity on the campus can lead to some traumatic clashes, Bowen declared, "I believe that the political and social fabric of this country requires that individuals of different races be educated in settings where they can learn how to learn from each other." By the time Bowen spoke, Asian-Americans, who have been growing rapidly in university admissions in recent years, nearly equaled African-American students in the new freshman class for the first time, and Hispanic-American students were not far behind the two larger groups of minority students.

In 1994 Princeton adopted an official statement of its commitment to diversity, declaring, "We actively seek students, faculty and staff of exceptional ability and promise who share in our commitment to excellence in teaching and scholarship and who will bring a diversity of viewpoints and cultures." That fall minority and foreign students comprised nearly one-third of the 1,158 members of the incoming class of 1998: 11.9 percent were Asian-American; 6.8 percent were African-American; 6.0 percent were Hispanic; and 11 students, about one percent, were

Minority Enrollment

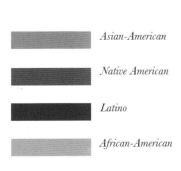

Asian-American

Native American

Latino

African-American

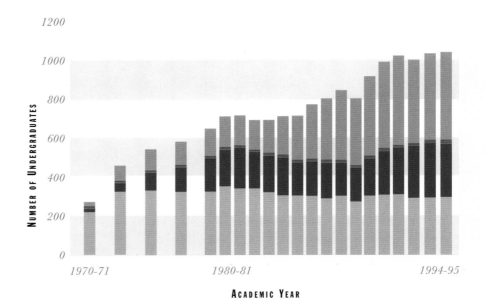

NUMBER OF UNDERGRADUATES

1200

1000

800

600

400

200

0

1970-71   1980-81   1994-95

ACADEMIC YEAR

Native American. An additional 6.0 percent were international students from 33 countries other than the United States. Based on estimates from available surveys (religion is no longer asked on application forms), about one-fourth of the class was Roman Catholic and around 10 percent was Jewish. More members of the Class of 1998 prepared for Princeton at public high schools (56.2 percent) than parochial schools (8.2 percent) or other private schools (35.5 percent).

Bringing demographic diversity to the ranks of the faculty has proven to be a more difficult challenge. As of 1994-95 only 12 percent of the full-time faculty was from minority groups, and the lion's share of these (nine percent) were Asian-American. Faculty leaders have vowed to do better in recruiting and appointing excellent minority candidates and in expanding the pool of qualified applicants by encouraging more minority students to pursue the Ph.D. While more remains to be done, on every side today's Princeton is more diverse than ever before.

Over time, increased diversity on campus has led to increased diversity in Princeton's alumni ranks.

Financial Underpinnings

PRINCETON'S FINANCIAL SIDE HAS HAD A HISTORY ALMOST AS COLORFUL AS THAT OF THE UNIVERSITY ITSELF.

S*taffers Jessie Serrell, Charlotte Nelms and Audrey Weiss sort incoming mail in February 1951 during the 11th Annual Giving campaign.*

M*oses Taylor Pyne, Class of 1877, with his only grandchild, Agnes. A man of great inherited wealth, Pyne devoted most of his adult life, and much of his fortune, to helping Princeton grow from a college into a university.*

Two years after the College of New Jersey was founded in 1746, a trustee of the fledgling school declared that "the principal thing we now want is a proper fund to enable us to go on with this expensive undertaking." Ever since, Princeton's financial side has had a history almost as colorful as that of the university itself.

In 1750 Benjamin Franklin was hired to print lottery tickets for the benefit of the college. Unfortunately this and several other lotteries proved not very profitable. Early individual donors included John Hancock, who gave the college £167 in 1769; George Washington, who gave 50 guineas in 1783; and James Madison, the first president of the alumni association, who bequeathed the college $1,000 out of the proceeds from the publication of his notes on the Constitutional Convention.

In 1853 a permanent endowment fund was created, but systematic fund-raising on the modern scale did not begin until the Annual Giving appeal to all alumni was established in 1940. The first year $80,000 was received. This has grown exponentially to the point that the 55th Annual Giving campaign closed in June 1995 with gifts totaling $21,170,663 in unrestricted funds. More than 56 percent of all alumni contributed to that campaign. Among living undergraduate alumni, more than 88 percent have contributed to Annual Giving at one time or another—a riveting testimony to their confidence in and loyalty to the university.

A series of development campaigns, as well as individual appeals to support special projects, have provided other forms of support to the modern Princeton. A $53 million campaign

Andrew Carnegie views his "loch" during its first crew regatta in 1907. His gift to Princeton involved not only water, but hundreds of acres of adjacent real estate which eventually provided the university with much-needed room to grow.

Invitation to testimonial dinner for C.C. Cuyler, Class of 1879, Princeton benefactor and trustee.

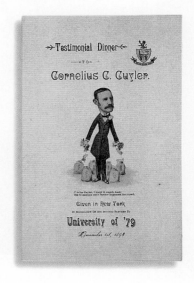

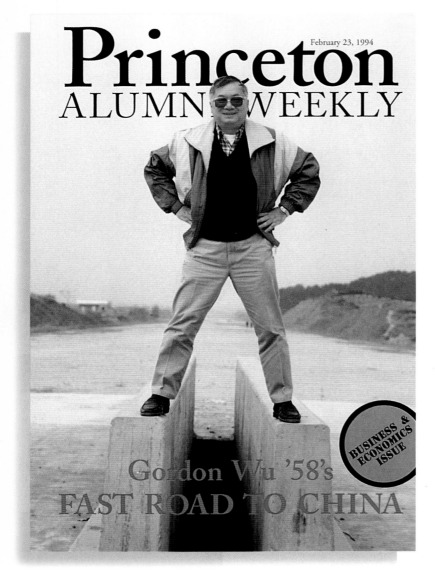

The February 23, 1994, issue of the Princeton Alumni Weekly *featured a profile of Hong Kong business tycoon Gordon Wu '58. Known around the world for his mammoth construction projects in Hong Kong, China and throughout Southeast Asia, Wu has become one of Princeton's all-time leading benefactors.*

launched in 1959 quickly exceeded its goal. A successor development program in the 1970s raised $125 million. A Campaign for Princeton, launched in 1981 with a goal of raising $275 million, actually raised $410 million by its termination in 1986.

Among the many extraordinary gifts were the original 4.5-acre plot given by Nathaniel FitzRandolph in 1753, on which Nassau Hall and the original campus were built, and the 3.5-mile-long lake given by Andrew Carnegie in 1906. Gifts in recent years have included $35 million given, at first anonymously, to the Woodrow Wilson School of Public and International Affairs by Mr. and Mrs. Charles Robertson '26 in 1961, when the annual operating budget of the university, other than externally sponsored research, was considerably less than that; and the $27 million bequest of Mrs. Stanley Palmer Jadwin in 1965 in memory of her son, L. Stockwell Jadwin '28, which was used to build and endow Jadwin Gym and the math-physics center dominated by Jadwin Hall and Fine Hall.

Due to generations of gifts and shrewd financial management, Princeton's endowment has reached $3.6 billion. The legendary Dean Mathey '12, a successful New York investment banker and long-time trustee, quietly moved the university's endowment out of stocks and into bonds in 1928, a year before the 1929 crash. In 1942 he reversed the action, selling the bonds and buying common stocks in time to catch the post-World War II boom. Due to a loan from university funds to Ray Kroc, the founder of McDonald's, Princeton in the early 1950s received a share of the proceeds of every hamburger sold under the golden arches.

In recent years the performance of Princeton's endowment has consistently ranked close to the top among universities. In 1994-95 the investment earnings from the endowment supported 29 percent of the overall university budget (excluding the Plasma Physics Laboratory, which is financed almost entirely by the federal government). Private sector gifts, including Annual Giving, supported 12 percent of the budget. Student tuition and fees, although painfully high by the standards of most families, made up only 28 percent of operating income.

Despite its massive endowment, excellent financial management, and the strong and continuous support of its alumni, parents and other contributors, Princeton as a private research university strongly committed to undergraduate teaching has entered a period of financial stringency, when it is forced to make increasingly difficult choices to maintain its high standards.

A 250th anniversary fund-raising campaign, which is aimed at strengthening Princeton's core programs, sustaining its commitment to financial aid, providing a new campus center, replacing Palmer Stadium and meeting a variety of other needs, is to be launched officially in the fall of 1995.

*P*hotograph of a casual Dean Mathey '12 that hangs in the master's office of Mathey College. The legendary investment banker moved Princeton out of stocks in 1928 and into hamburgers in the early 1950s.

1914 *football program from the day Palmer Stadium was dedicated. The score mimicked the year, 19-14, but unfortunately for the Tigers, the 19 belonged to Yale.*

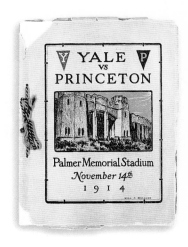

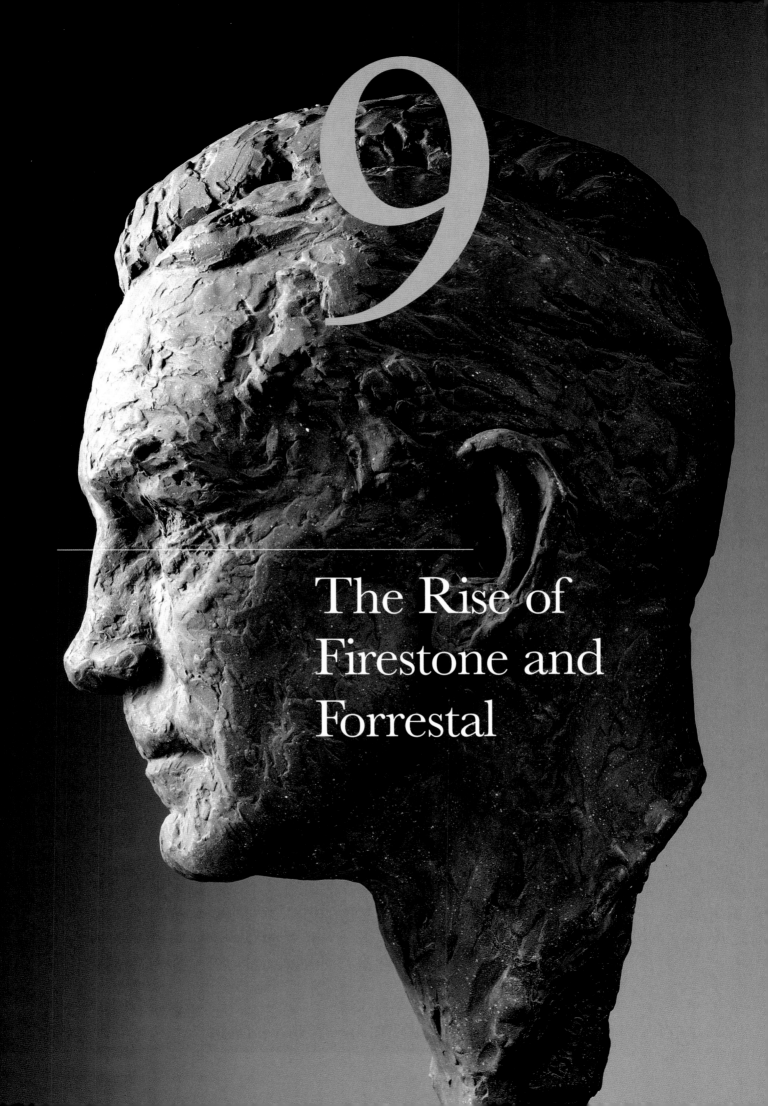

The Rise of Firestone and Forrestal

Busts (previous pages) of Harvey S. Firestone (left) in the main foyer of the library that bears his name, and James V. Forrestal '15 in the reading room of the Seeley G. Mudd Manuscript Library.

1959 *experimental air cushion vehicle, from an exhibition at the Forrestal Research Center.*

As Princeton was adjusting to the post-World War II era, two great complexes were added that became operating centers as well as imposing symbols of a new age in academic research. One was Firestone Library, opened in 1948 and formally dedicated in 1949, a "laboratory for the humanities" that quickly became a central academic resource as well as a study hall for many undergraduates and graduate students. The other was the Forrestal Research Center, located three miles away from the rest of the campus on property purchased in 1951, which became a laboratory for high-technology research in aeronautical, mechanical and nuclear fields, with operating funds provided predominantly by the U.S. government.

The rise to prominence of Firestone and Forrestal in the postwar era reflected a commitment to scholarship and research that dates back to the earliest days of the university. Presidents Witherspoon and McCosh emphasized scholarly work in the humanities, and both identified books and the library as crucial assets in that mission. The tradition of scientific research at Princeton dates back to Witherspoon's purchase of the Rittenhouse Orrery in 1771. Experimental science began with the work of Joseph Henry, who sent perhaps the world's first telegraph signal across the Princeton campus in 1836 to tell his household he was ready for lunch.

Throughout much of Princeton's history the interaction between the search for new knowledge and the transmission of existing knowledge was recognized as crucial to the university's educational mission. Professor Theodore J. Ziolkowski, dean of

How short the space between two cardinal points of an earthly career!—the point of birth and that of death; and yet what a universe of wonders is presented to us in our rapid flight through this space! Joseph Henry

the graduate school from 1979 to 1992, wrote that "it is the dedication to scholarship and research—the commitment to the process of knowledge rather than merely to its product—that contributes the intellectual tension and excitement to life in a university. It is scholarship that makes of Princeton a major world university and not simply—as fine as it may be—an undergraduate college that transmits knowledge."

*W*oodcut of Firestone Library.

Books and the library were major concerns of the founders of Princeton and other American colleges. Governor Jonathan Belcher's gift of 474 volumes from his personal library in 1755 marked the beginning of the college collection and the start of a passion for collected knowledge that has never flagged. As early as 1760 President Samuel Davies published a catalog of 1,281 volumes as a fund-raising venture to obtain more books. Davies wrote, in words that continue to be apt:

A large and well-sorted Collection of Books on the various Branches of Literature is… the most proper and valuable Fund with which [a college] can be endowed. It is one of the best Helps to enrich the Minds both of the Officers and Students with Knowledge; to give them an extensive Acquaintance with Authors; and to lead them beyond the narrow Limits of the Books to which they are confined in their stated Studies and Recitations, that they may expatiate at large thro' the boundless and variegated Fields of Science [i.e., knowledge].

On June 16, 1947, on behalf of his mother and his four brothers, all of whom were Princeton alumni, Harvey S. Firestone, Jr., '20 laid the cornerstone for the new library as President Dodds looked on.

The original college library in Nassau Hall survived the damages of the Revolutionary War but was nearly destroyed in the fire of 1802. Reestablished and enlarged, the library acquired its first separate building, the Chancellor Green Library (part of the present student center), in 1873. The Pyne Library (now East Pyne) was constructed in 1897 to accommodate the fast-growing collection, which was then approaching 200,000 books. By the 1920s the need for much more space was evident.

When Firestone Library was planned in the 1940s, it was described as a new type of "laboratory for the humanities."

"Statue" at Princeton University, Princeton, N. J.

Rather than being a giant warehouse for books that could only be called forth by readers from librarians, one by one, to a poorly lighted reading room, Firestone was designed to be different. After obtaining access to the library, readers would find its stacks open to browsers as well as scholars, with books on any subject grouped together on the shelves. At its opening Firestone was the first large open-stack university library in the world. Added to the convenience of this revolutionary design were study spaces, including special reading rooms and tables scattered among the shelves as well as private study carrels available to thesis-writing seniors and graduate students.

When my class entered Princeton in the fall of 1948, Firestone was just being opened for use, though it was not officially dedicated until the following year. We used it heavily and consistently. The *Daily Princetonian* during the year when I was chairman (i.e., editor-in-chief) carried on an impassioned campaign against a plan to shut down Firestone at 10:00 p.m. instead of midnight to

Paleontologists combing the Firestone excavation for fossils made a number of important discoveries, including this "Library Fossil."

*"T*he Tyger," a poem by *William Blake from* Songs of Innocence and Experience: Shewing the Two Contrary States of the Human Soul. *Blake hand-lettered and painted this self-published edition, which appeared in 1794. It is in the Caroline Newton Collection in Firestone's rare books.*

Treasures of Firestone Library

*H*ead of Alexander the *Great (top) on a late 4th-century B.C. tetradrachma, and a coin from the brief reign of the Roman emperor Macrinus, 217-18 A.D. These are two of over 8,000 Greek and Roman coins in the Firestone numismatics collection.*

*W*illiam Scheide '36 *studies his Gutenberg Bible in the Scheide Library, located within Firestone. As this photograph was being taken, he discovered a typographical error in the Latin text.*

save money. We called it a false economy for a university whose library had become an essential resource for its students. In the end Nassau Hall canceled the plan.

Today Firestone, together with its 18 subsidiary branches in various locations on campus and its storage annex at Forrestal, contains more than five million printed books, two million microfilms and other reduced-size microforms, 30,000 current periodicals, and a large number of manuscripts and other materials in special collections. As of 1993 the Princeton library system ranked 16th in size among university collections in the United States and Canada and eighth among the 119 members of the Association of Research Libraries in the number of books purchased (about 100,000 volumes per year). To accommodate the ever-growing collection and a persistent demand for better study space, a major addition to Firestone was completed in 1988. On average, 86 books are checked out annually by each student and faculty member—a remarkable testament to the library's usefulness and scholarly importance. Firestone's entire catalog of books is now on computer.

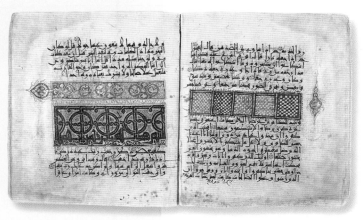

When Saudi Arabian Crown Prince Saud al ibn Saud and retinue visited Firestone in 1947 (top), Near Eastern Studies Professor Philip Hitti showed the Prince a Koran from the Garrett Collection. Bottom: A 12th-century Eastern Kufic Koran, also from the Garrett Collection.

In recent years computers have joined books as an essential resource for teaching and research in all areas of the university. The use of computing in research, teaching and administration escalated rapidly after Princeton established its first computer center in the Engineering Quadrangle in 1962 to house an IBM 7090. In 1969 the university constructed a Computing Center building at 87 Prospect Avenue and

Physics professors (l-r) Henry Smyth '18, John Wheeler and Eugene Wigner examine a sample of "jade" (below) from the melted sand at Alamogordo, New Mexico, site of Trinity, the first nuclear detonation in history.

installed an IBM 360/91. Since then the university has expanded access to computing and information technology by constructing a campus-wide telecommunications network. By 1994 nearly 80 percent of all undergraduates had their own computers, and more than 7,500 campus computers were connected to the network.

While Firestone was being opened in the late 1940s as the central resource for the social sciences and humanities, the research requirements of the physical sciences and engineering were entering a demanding new phase.

During World War II, according to Physics department chairman Henry DeWolf Smyth '18, every member of Princeton's world-renowned Physics department was released from teaching for war research either in Princeton or elsewhere. Key members of the department joined the Manhattan Project at Los Alamos, the secret operation that produced the first atomic bomb. The sudden secret exodus of university physicists to New Mexico puzzled Princeton residents until news of the A-bomb was revealed in 1945.

In 1944, even before the war was over, Smyth reported to President Dodds, "The university must choose between going ahead vigorously, capitalizing on the fine record of this department during the war or letting its physicists drift away to such a degree that it may take a generation to restore the department. The first course will require money for men and for equipment, a great deal of money, but it offers a magnificent opportunity, completely in the tradition of the university. We have never been in a better position to push forward in the field of fundamental physical research."

The U.S. government, which in the Manhattan Project had seen what wonders could be produced by the organized collaboration of scientific, technical, administrative and manufacturing capabilities, continued to sponsor research after World War II ended and the Cold War began. The post-World War II Physics department began receiving large grants for research in cosmic rays, shock waves and other topics from the newly created Atomic Energy Commission and the Office of Naval Research. The department of

PRINCETON ENGINEER

REPORT FROM EUROPE
SCATTER TRANSMISSION
THE CASE FOR CONCRETE HIGHWAYS

SYNCHROTRON: PRINCETON'S NEW ATOM SMASHER

OCTOBER, 1956

1956 *cover of the* Princeton Engineer *announcing the construction of the Princeton-Penn Accelerator on the Forrestal campus.*

P*rofessor Alexander Nikolsky testing an air cushion vehicle at a 1959 exhibition at Forrestal.*

AEROMOBILE

Aeronautical Engineering, whose Professor Alexander Nikolsky had helped design the first practical American helicopter, was awarded Navy contracts for basic and applied research on aircraft design, jet propulsion and the development of guided missiles. By 1949 the university was carrying on 63 different sponsored research projects in a wide variety of fields, with 37 of them supported by the government and the rest by foundations and industry.

After the Korean war broke out in June 1950, and especially after Chinese troops entered the war in November, both the prospects and the pressures for extensive government support in the physical sciences and engineering intensified. However, the experiments being proposed involved jet propulsion, shock waves and explosions, with resulting noise, dust and tremors that would disrupt the life of the campus.

In January 1951 Princeton announced the purchase of an 825-acre property, including numerous buildings and an air strip,

Secretary of Defense James V. Forrestal '15, pictured at his desk only a few weeks before his suicide in 1949.

that had been occupied by the Rockefeller Institute for Medical Research three miles away from the main campus across Route 1. Adding to the 600-acre main campus, it was the greatest single expansion of the university since its move to Princeton from Newark in 1756. New York newspapers referred to it as "the second Louisiana Purchase." Named in memory of James V. Forrestal '15, the nation's first secretary of defense, who had ended his life in a suicide two years before, the Forrestal Research Center was to be Princeton's space for large-scale science and engineering. In the face of serious questions about whether such a big new expansion project should be undertaken, President Dodds told the press, "The growing national emergency hastened the decision."

Prodded by John Wheeler, a respected and well-known Princeton professor of physics who had been working on the hydrogen bomb at Los Alamos and sought to continue his work at Princeton, the university agreed in 1951 to play host to top-secret H-bomb research at Forrestal because of the requirements of national defense in time of war. In a memo to the university's office of public relations, Wheeler described the public posture of

*O*n *February 22, 1950, an oil fire destroyed the 18-million-volt cyclotron in Palmer Physical Laboratory. This atom-smashing machine, which was being used for naval nuclear research, had previously been employed on the Manhattan Project.*

Professor Lyman Spitzer, Jr., *38 skiing at Mammoth, California, in 1960. He was an accomplished skier long before the sport became popular.

Technicians add helical windings to the racetrack-shaped Model C Stellarator in 1961. This plasma transporter was in operation until 1969, when it was converted to a tokamak reactor. In a tokamak, the plasma fuel is confined by a magnetic field within a hollow doughnut-shaped vacuum chamber.

the work he was heading at Forrestal as one of "complete silence." The government even insisted that President Dodds obtain a security clearance in order to be told the general outline of the secret work that would be taking place under university auspices. By 1953 the H-bomb work (code-named Project Matterhorn B) was moved to Los Alamos, and Princeton adopted policies to minimize (then in 1971 to prohibit) classified research.

Meanwhile, Princeton astrophysicist Lyman Spitzer, Jr., *38 had an inspiration on a ski slope in Colorado about the possibility that highly controlled thermonuclear fusion could be used as an inexhaustible source of energy. Unlike Matterhorn B, Spitzer's Project Matterhorn S concentrated on production of energy for civilian use. Physics chairman Smyth, who had promoted the project while on leave as a member of the Atomic Energy Commission in Washington, reported to the trustees in 1956 that "Princeton is now playing a leading role in exploring the most exciting and important technological possibility of our time.... Though success cannot be promised, Princeton has a good chance to produce controlled power from the fusion of hydrogen before anyone else in the world." The Atomic Energy Commission, he pointed out in the same report, would pay all direct and indirect costs.

Due largely to these projects and developments, government-sponsored research at Princeton, mostly at the Forrestal campus, increased by leaps and bounds, from $1.3 million in 1950-51 to $4.2 million in 1954-55 to $7.6 million in 1956-57 to $14.7 million in 1957-58. After the Soviet Union shocked the world in October 1957 by launching Sputnik, the first space satellite, the federal government sharply accelerated its support for higher education and sophisticated research. As a result the government doubled its support for research at Princeton in 1959-60, spending over $23 million at a time when income from student fees amounted to about $5 million, proceeds from endowment about $4.3 million and total operating income was $42 million.

In 1962 Professor (later President) William G. Bowen made the first comprehensive study of the impact of sponsored research at Princeton. While citing some dangers to the university, such as skewing its scholarly programs and graduate student support in favor of sponsored areas and the ever-present risk of a sharp decline in government funding, Bowen concluded that, on the whole, participation in research projects sponsored by government agencies,

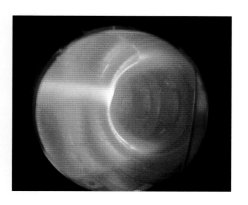

View of the Tokamak Fusion Test Reactor (TFTR) and (top) of an actual plasma in the reactor vessel. The heavy hydrogen in the plasma circulates at temperatures above 500,000,000 degrees celsius, or about 25 times as hot as the center of the sun.

foundations and industries "has had a profound positive effect on Princeton's ability to fulfill both her teaching and research objectives." He added, "It is hard to imagine what the scientific side of the university would look like today in the absence of government programs."

1993 *Nobel laureate in physics, Russell Hulse, in the control room of the Plasma Physics Laboratory's Tokamak Fusion Test Reactor.*

Gradually, however, the scientific prominence of the Forrestal research campus declined. Flight research was phased out as government and industry support decreased and the encroachment of commercial development placed restrictions on operations. The big Princeton-Penn accelerator, a huge device of coils, cables and magnets built to hurl subatomic particles at high speeds, was shut down in 1972 following the transfer of funding to newer and bigger machines elsewhere. In 1988 the once-famed experimental machine and its outbuildings were razed by bulldozers and wrecking balls. Some of the Forrestal research property was added to a university-sponsored commercial development project of offices, hotels, residences and retail establishments that had been initiated in 1973.

The Forrestal lands not converted to commercial use continue to support research and some administrative functions of the university. One of the buildings at Forrestal houses the federally sponsored Geophysical Fluid Dynamics Laboratory, which has close ties to the university's engineering school and its department of Geological and Geophysical Sciences. But the Forrestal project with the longest record of accomplishment is Project Matterhorn's successor, the Princeton Plasma Physics Laboratory (PPPL), which continues to pursue its ambitious aim of developing thermonuclear fusion as an inexhaustible, safe, economical and environmentally acceptable means of generating electricity in the next century. Funded by the U.S. Department of Energy at a level of roughly $100 million a year, the PPPL reactor in 1993 and 1994 broke all previous records for production of energy from controlled fusion.

By 1994 the university's total budget for sponsored research, apart from PPPL, was $83 million, spread over 1,054 projects in essentially all the disciplines represented at Princeton. (This compared to a total university budget, again excluding PPPL, of $411 million.) Of this outside funding, some 77 percent came from the government, 10 percent from industry, seven percent from foundations and six percent from other sources.

Computer model from the Geophysical Fluid Dynamics Laboratory (GFDL) at the Forrestal campus depicts variations in surface temperature of a rotating fluid flow over a mountain.

High resolution GFDL circulation model, dubbed the SKYHI, simulates three-dimensional air motions and their impact on atmospheric chemistry. An understanding of the mixing of air between the polar vortex (depicted here) and lower latitudes is important for predicting the impact of polar ozone losses.

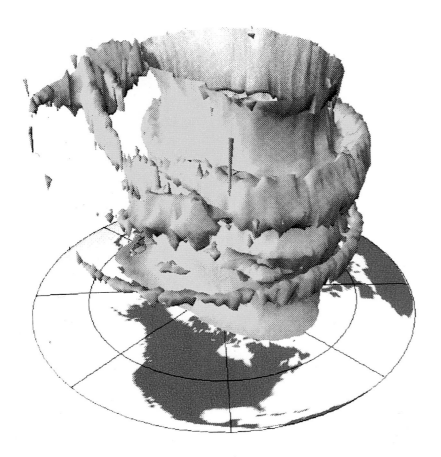

Robert F. Goheen, 1957-72

"LIBERAL EDUCATION IS, IN THE MOST ESSENTIAL WAY, EDUCATION FOR USE— NEVER MORE CRITICALLY SO THAN IN TIMES SUCH AS OURS."

An alumnus of both the undergraduate college and the graduate school, Robert Goheen presided over a major building program, made possible by the highly successful $53 million campaign of the early 1960s and a substantial increase in federal funding for research.

Born: Vengurla, India, 1919. B.A., Princeton, 1940. Ph.D. in Classics, Princeton, 1948.

The son of a Presbyterian medical missionary, Robert Goheen was a 37-year-old assistant professor of classics when he bowled over a trustee committee seeking a successor to Harold Dodds. In view of Goheen's relative youth and lack of seniority, choosing him as president was "one of the most courageous things I ever did," recalled Harold H. Helm '20, a leader of the committee that interviewed him. The trustees promoted Goheen to full professor at the same time they elected him to the presidency.

Goheen presided over the era of most rapid change, and perhaps of greatest stress, in the modern history of the university. Under his leadership Princeton became coeducational, greatly expanded its admission of black students and dealt with the protests arising from the Vietnam war, in part by giving students a more influential voice in the governance of the university. The annual budget quadrupled from about $20 million to $80 million under his administration, and 25 new buildings sprang up on the main campus, in addition to others at the Graduate College and Forrestal Research Center.

A calm and deliberate leader who won praise for his ability to listen, Goheen declared in his inaugural address in 1957, "Liberal education is not a luxury item which a free society can well afford to surrender, or even much dilute. Liberal education is, in the most essential way, education for use—never more critically so than in times such as ours. The complexities of modern life put great pressures on individuals to abrogate responsibility. Too often the way out, when faced with private or public dilemmas, seems to be to surrender to instinct and unfettered emotion."

After resigning the presidency, Goheen went on to be president of the Council on Foundations, U.S. ambassador to India, director of the Mellon Fellowships in the Humanities program and a senior fellow at the Woodrow Wilson School.

Goheen, being interviewed here in 1958 by Edward R. Murrow, was nationally respected for his leadership of Princeton, especially during the upheavals of the late 1960s and early 1970s.

Perhaps foreshadowing the maelstrom at the end of the decade, the 1960s began with a visit from Hurricane Donna. Goheen (right) surveys the damage with Financial Vice President Ricardo Mestres '31.

10

Coeducation

Princeton women at 1988 commencement (previous page), from the catalog for a spring 1990 Firestone Library exhibit on Gender in the Academy, marking the 20th anniversary of undergraduate coeducation.

By coincidence the female tiger of a bronze pair by sculptor Bruce Moore was lowered into place next to Clio Hall in September 1969, within a week of the arrival of Princeton's first female undergraduates. The male-female set had been ordered long before coeducation was contemplated.

O n a May afternoon in 1967, *Daily Princetonian* reporter Robert Durkee '69 had an appointment with President Goheen, one of a regular monthly series to keep the undergraduate newspaper informed of Nassau Hall's thinking. When Durkee raised the subject of coeducation, Goheen responded that "It is inevitable that, at some point in the future, Princeton is going to move into the education of women. The only questions now are those of strategy, priority and timing."

Durkee was startled by the reply, which foreshadowed a fundamental change in Princeton's all-male history and tradition. His story dominated the front page of the May 17 issue of the *Prince* and quickly became the talk of the campus. It also stunned Goheen, who was under the impression that his thinking-out-loud about the future was not for publication, and in any case did not anticipate the powerful, almost explosive, impact it would have on the Princeton community.

Goheen had taken a public position in 1965 that "Princeton has no problems coeducation would cure," but by 1967 he had been quietly rethinking his stand. When he recruited William G. Bowen to be his provost, Bowen, a product of coeducational high schools and coeducational Denison University, cautioned that "I think the all-male Princeton cannot be, it cannot last." Goheen did not yet accept that conclusion but asked only that Bowen express his view in private, rather than in public.

Around this time admission officers were concerned about a falling off in accep-

F. EARL CHRISTY

tances of offers of admission to Princeton and were telling Goheen that some of the brightest applicants increasingly were choosing to go elsewhere because of the absence of women on campus. Shortly before meeting with the student reporter, Goheen received a letter from William L. Pressly '31, headmaster of Westminster Schools in Atlanta, saying the all-male environment was a major reason why no students from his school would be coming to Princeton that fall.

Meanwhile, Yale had opened well-publicized discussions about the possible move of all-female Vassar College to all-male Yale. In light of this, Goheen had told the trustees confidentially in January 1967 that "Princeton in a few years might find itself the only major university not significantly engaged in the education of women" and at a serious competitive disadvantage because of this fact. He had put the trustees on notice that he was actively working on the issue and would be ready to discuss his thinking at a subsequent board meeting. In fact, he began tentatively exploring a possible merger of Princeton with Sarah Lawrence College in Bronxville, New York, but eventually both sides dropped the idea.

On June 12, the day before the 1967 commencement and the 10th anniversary of his assumption of the presidency, Goheen brought the coeducation issue to the trustees in what would prove to be a historic meeting. "In my judgment, the time has now come when it can no longer be reckoned to Princeton's advantage to postpone entry into the education of women on a significant scale," Goheen declared. He gave three major reasons: the potentially negative effect on Princeton admissions as coeducation proceeded elsewhere; the positive effect that the presence of women would have on the intellectual and cultural life of the university; and, above all, the "more extensive and active role of women in the modern world and their rising need for the best in higher education." Beyond the requirement to keep up with the times, Goheen said, "a university with so profound a sense of obligation to the world can no longer, I believe, ignore the educational needs of one half of the human race."

In the discussion that followed, most of the trustees seemed sympathetic to admitting women, but there were serious questions about its practicality. Goheen did not ask them to approve such an important departure from tradition immediately. Instead, he asked for approval of an extensive and objective study under Gardner Patterson, a highly respected professor of economics, of the desirability and feasibility of coeducation at the undergraduate level. A year later Patterson presented the trustees with his 288-page report, "The Education of Women at

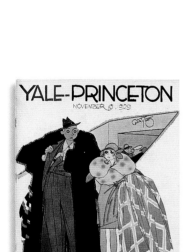

1929 *cover of the Yale game football program. By the "Roaring '20s," tight corsets, hand muffs and floor-length dresses had given way to the more comfortable and revealing flapper style.*

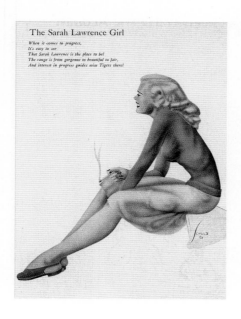

The Sarah Lawrence Girl

When it comes to progress,
It's easy to see
That Sarah Lawrence is the place to be!
The range is from gorgeous to beautiful to fair,
And interest in progress guides wise Tigers there!

Princeton," in which had been enlisted an impressive faculty-administration committee. The study concluded that coeducation at Princeton was desirable and feasible and that admission of women with a goal of at least 1,000 women undergraduates should begin as soon as possible.

Knowing that there would be strong resistance by tradition-minded men, Goheen asked Harold H. Helm '20, a longtime trustee and former chairman of the trustees' executive committee, to head a trustee committee to study the Patterson report. Helm recalled years later, "I immediately said to him, 'Bob, I think you've got the wrong man. I am not very keen about the [coeducation] idea…. I enjoy Princeton too much as it is and like it so well that I think it would be hard for me to accept so radical a change.'" Goheen responded, "I didn't ask you to vote for it; I asked you to study it." Helm agreed to do so with an open mind. In the end his trustee committee, with Laurance S. Rockefeller '32 as vice-chairman, endorsed coeducation and helped raise the money to finance it.

Evelyn College

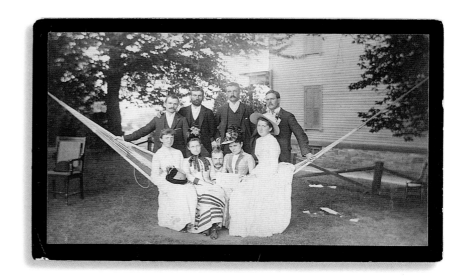

Founded in 1887 by former Princeton professor Joshua Hall McIlvaine, Class of 1837, the college was named for Sir John Evelyn, a 17th-century English literary figure. Its opening led Harper's Bazaar to predict that "our country shall come to speak with equal pride of the sons and daughters of Princeton." Evelyn's enrollment, never more than 50 a year, consisted largely of daughters of college and seminary professors and sisters of Princeton students. When McIlvaine died in 1897, during a period of economic depression in America, he had failed to secure an adequate endowment for his school, and Evelyn College closed its doors forever. The college building (below) still stands as a private residence.

Evelyn was wildly popular with Princeton men. By renting its first house next to the college, the newly formed Colonial Club immediately strengthened its competitive position against the four older eating clubs—Ivy, Cottage, Tiger Inn and Cap and Gown. Left: An Evelyn College dance card.

On January 11, 1969, by a 24-8 show of hands in the Faculty Room of Nassau Hall, the trustees agreed that Princeton should open its doors to women as regular members of the undergraduate body. Three months later the trustees approved the implementation plans, and Goheen announced that the first women would join the student body in September. That night WPRB, the campus radio station, concluded its broadcast of the big news with a stirring rendition of the "Hallelujah Chorus."

Although the trustees called it "the largest single decision that has faced Princeton in this century," the move to admit women had a lengthy history.

From 1887 to 1897 Evelyn College, a private college for women, operated near Harrison and Nassau streets. Princeton professors, including President Patton, taught at Evelyn, but the students did not attend classes at the all-male Princeton college. Socially, however, Evelyn was a great success at football games, at eating club parties and in some cases at the marriage altar with Princeton men. Special police patrolled the women's dormitories, but "Eva, Eva, l-y-n, Eva, Eva, let me in!" was a frequent Princeton rallying cry, according to local historians.

Half a century later the first female students arrived at the campus as photogrammetry trainees during World War II when Princeton was largely taken over by military agencies. They were not admitted as degree students, however.

The first major step came in the early 1960s when the graduate school was permitted to admit a limited number of highly qualified women "for whom Princeton offers special or particular opportunities." Up to that point, the trustees were

During World War II 23 women were admitted into a government-sponsored defense course in photogrammetry.

Professor Phillip Kissam (above) instructs Frances Jones and Marjorie Miller. Below: Lieutenant Howard Schnur and Marian J. Stock.

*I*n 1961 Mrs. Sabra Follett Meservey, a faculty member at Douglass College in New Brunswick, became the first woman Ph.D. candidate admitted to Princeton. She received her degree in 1966.

told, Princeton was the only university in the country that did not accept women for graduate work; at all other Ivy League schools women comprised around 20 percent of graduate students. In 1961, with the new ruling in place, Mrs. Sabra F. Meservey, a Princeton resident who had been a college-level faculty member elsewhere, was admitted to the graduate school as the first female Ph.D. student, in Oriental Studies. Some trustees worried that admitting Meservey might be "letting the camel get its nose under the tent," Goheen recalled.

Another crack in the closed door came in 1963 when Princeton agreed to enroll a limited number of undergraduate women as temporary transfer students studying "critical languages" (including Chinese, Japanese, Arabic and Russian) under a new Carnegie Corporation program. The critical language students, or "critters" as they were known, received degrees from their home institutions rather than from Princeton.

In the mid-1960s a steadily rising undergraduate demand for the admission of women was evident in *Daily Princetonian* editorials and special articles. At the same time, there was also strong resistance to change on the part of many students and a substantial part of the alumni body, who cited tradition in insisting that

*T*he critical language students of 1967-68 pose for the Bric-a-Brac at their residence on Library Place. The yearbook quoted one as observing that "the humor of seeing Tigers on weekdays without their stripes of tweed, gawking and adolescently tongue-tied, avoiding the seats next to us in class, was countered by the bittersweet of seeing our weekday friends become weekend snowmen trying to impress imports at club parties."

Princeton should retain its all-male status. One alumnus wrote to the *Alumni Weekly* that "the Princeton student who does not have women in his classes, lectures and preceptorials enjoys four years of a developing manhood uncluttered by the trivia and fluff of those women who will later share in the rest of his life." Another expressed his views in a poem:

So, to the nutty notions
Which feed the campus squirrels
Let's add the last, which takes the prize,
And let in all the girls.

When the trustees made their decision in January 1969, they presented Director of Admission John Osander '57 with an unusual and vexing problem. The trustees had decided "in principle" to admit women for the first time, but no one was sure how soon the university would be ready to take this momentous step in practice. In February Osander wrote to guidance counselors throughout the country inviting applications from women with the understanding "that we may not be able to admit any freshmen women this year." In response, 505 women immediately applied for places in Princeton's freshman class. As the moment of decision approached, Osander drew up two sets of letters for the 130 women who had won the approval of the Admission Office. One set of letters began, "We regret to inform you that Princeton University does not accept women." These were later used for scrap paper. The other set

Snowball fight during student-initiated "Coed Week," February 1969.

Male and female black squirrels (Sciurus niger), fabled on campus for their "Princeton colors," from John James Audubon's Viviparous Quadrupeds of North America, among Firestone's rare books.

announced the exciting news that the applicant had been accepted as a Princeton student beginning in September.

Robin Herman '73, who went on to become a *Daily
Princetonian* editor and one of the nation's first female sportswrit-
ers, recalled that "it was around 6:00 a.m." when the news of the
Princeton trustees' decision reached her home. "My father heard
it on the radio. He came and woke me up and told me I had to
apply." Writing in the *Alumni Weekly* 10 years after her graduation,
Herman recalled, "From the start, the women of '73 were a
group apart. Marked by the circumstances of the school's history,
they are in many ways unique even among Princeton women
after them. They applied to a school that at the time was closed
to women, and they entered a risky situation as part of what some
people viewed as an experiment."

Macie Green '73, another coeducational pioneer, said, "I
promised my father [who was a Princeton alumnus] that if
Princeton went coed, I'd apply." Many other female applicants
had no previous connection with Princeton but found the idea of
blazing a new trail for women at a great university exciting and

attractive. "There aren't that many opportunities to be first at anything anymore," said Anita Fefer '73. While nearly all the pioneering women found their undergraduate years a challenge, most of them did not wish to change Princeton in any fundamental sense, but rather to be part of it. "I want to be involved here," Jean Berner '73 told the *Daily Princetonian*. "I want to be able to say this is my school."

At first the women were housed in Pyne Hall, a relatively isolated dormitory near the train station. Worried administrators placed special locks on the entry doors. "Most of the girls in my own entry are as irritated as I am, simply because it's not fun to feel like a bloody gold brick stuffed away in a corner of Fort Knox," wrote Mary Azoy '71, who had transferred as a junior from Bradford Junior College, in the diary she kept at the time. At another point a special security system of buzzers and an intercom was rigged up at Pyne, but the women deliberately broke it within a day. "We did not want to be cloistered," one recalled. The university took the hint. By the beginning of the

June Fletcher '73 (center) attracted intense media attention when she enrolled at Princeton in the fall of 1969 after being elected that summer's Miss Bikini USA. Below: Exterior of Pyne Hall, home of all women undergraduates, September 1969.

I think you need a lot more than formal learning in order to be a civilized being.

SUZANNE KELLER, SOCIOLOGIST, FIRST TENURED WOMAN FACULTY MEMBER

Sue Jean Lee and eight other critical language students transferred to Princeton for their senior years and graduated as members of the Class of 1970, becoming the first nine women to receive Princeton undergraduate degrees. Lee was also the first woman to join the cast of Triangle, performing in this 1968-69 production of A Different Kick.

At Princeton's 1975 commencement, the valedictory address was given by Cynthia Chase (left) and the Latin salutatory by Lisa Siegman. It was the first time in Princeton's history that the faculty had awarded either honor to a woman.

third year of coeducation, women had spread out to 11 separate dorms, all without extra locks or special restrictions.

Although at first women were a tiny minority—less than five percent of the undergraduates the first year and only 11 percent the second—many of them enthusiastically joined in the life of the campus. By the end of the second year of coeducation, six women were among the 16 new journalists joining the staff of the *Daily Princetonian*, the vice president of the Undergraduate Assembly was a woman, and a large number of other campus organizations, including the Triangle Club, included women as full participants. In the Triangle show that spring a scene of Princeton Charlies picking up their dates at the Junction for a big weekend featured, in line with Triangle tradition, male students portraying the imported lovelies in their flowered dresses. But this year, beneath their tailored jackets, the Princeton Charlies were women.

Not everything went smoothly. In April 1971 two women were placed on probation for entering the nearby room of a male student at 11:30 p.m. and ripping down the nude pinups that covered his walls. A student-faculty disciplinary committee considered the act "a serious infringement of important personal rights," turning a deaf ear to the argument of one of the women that destruction of the pinups was "in a tradition of political disobedience that goes back to Thoreau and Gandhi."

Without wishing to spray any moss—or demean the young selves that I and my contemporaries can still feel within us—I would nonetheless suggest that the ambience of the campus, including the classroom, has changed forever, and forever for the good.   JOHN MCPHEE '53 ON COEDUCATION

As momentous as coeducation was for Princeton, these were also tumultuous times for the country. "It would be misleading to suggest that coeducation was the event of 1969-70. Bigger issues—the war in Vietnam, the first draft lottery, the Kent State killings, the strike [a nationwide campus demonstration against the Vietnam war]—helped keep our minor tribulations in perspective," recalled Gail Finney '73. These events, which were the focus of life on the Princeton campus, helped make it possible for men and women to work together on common and transcendent causes.

An important step in the coeducational process was the trustees' decision in January 1974 to eliminate numerical quotas for men and women. Initially, the university had said that the number of men entering as freshmen each year—approximately 800—would not decline because of the admission of women, who would constitute a net increase in the size of the student body. The resulting quota system for men and women came under heavy criticism in the 1973 report of the Commission on

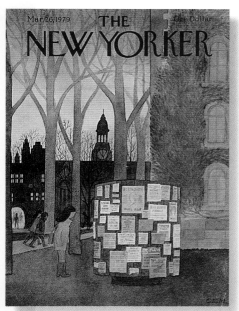

1979 New Yorker *cover cartoon depicting a woman student reading an information kiosk in what by then had become a normal campus scene (with a certain amount of artistic license on the arrangement of the architecture).*

the Future of the College, headed by Professor Marvin Bressler, which pointed out that such quotas might be illegal as well as unfair as a matter of principle. The faculty, the Undergraduate Assembly and the Executive Committee of the Alumni Council all endorsed the new policy of "equal access" before its adoption by the trustees. "Princeton's commitment to the pursuit of excellence...entails an obligation to admit the best students available," said Andrew Strenio '74, president of the Undergraduate Assembly, in a presentation to the trustees, "not the best 800 men and 300 women—but the best students, period."

In June 1975, when only the third fully coed class took its place in caps and gowns for commencement, both the valedictorian and the salutatorian were women. In general, though, "men and women students have achieved essentially identical results" in terms of academic perfor-

Liz Fagan '95 celebrates a goal as the 1994 women's lacrosse team beats the University of Maryland 10-7 to win the NCAA national championship. A week later the men's lacrosse team also won its national title.

Molly Marcoux '91, four-year All-Ivy women's hockey player, graduated as Princeton's all-time leading scorer. In 1990 she was one of 12 women selected for the Eastern College Athletic Conference "Team of the Decade."

mance such as grades and honors, President Bowen reported in a retrospective study of the first decade of coeducation.

A professional survey of student views in 1989, two decades after the start of coeducation, reported that a large majority of undergraduate women (and men) were "satisfied" or "very satisfied" with their overall Princeton experience. Somewhat fewer, but still a large majority of both sexes, were satisfied with their social life. Nonetheless, many women still were not comfortable with the prevailing campus climate. More than one-third of them reported feeling isolated or alone "often" or "almost always" compared to one-fifth of their male counterparts. And many more women than men described sexual harass-

Undergraduate Enrollment By Gender

1883-84 THROUGH 1993-94

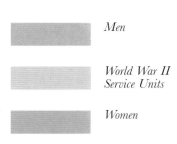

Men

World War II
Service Units

Women

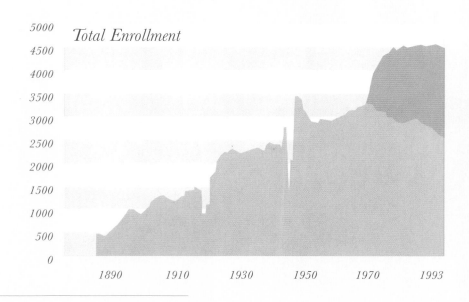

Total Enrollment

ment, racial harassment, harassment of gays and lesbians, and eating disorders as problems on campus.

The Class of 1998, which entered the university in September 1994, was 47.5 percent female, the highest percentage in Princeton history. For the first time, a majority of students planning to seek the bachelor of arts degree (51.2 percent) were women. (With encouragement from the engineering school and the Admission Office, the percentage of undergraduate women in engineering had reached 33 percent, a relatively high proportion by national standards.) In addition, 37 percent of graduate students were women, and as of 1994–95, 21 percent of the full-time faculty and 48 percent of the part-time faculty were women.

As anyone strolling across campus can attest, the days are long past when women were just dates for big weekends, or even a small minority of students. Over 25 years of coeducation, the women of Princeton have moved increasingly into the forefront of university life.

Women from the classes of 1997 and 1998 grapple during Cane Spree.

Susan Lynch '89 counsels children at the Princeton-Blairstown Center.

Princeton Athletes

In 1896 Robert Garrett organized and financed a four-man Princeton track team that traveled to Athens for the first modern Olympics. He was the most outstanding athlete of the games with a bronze, a silver

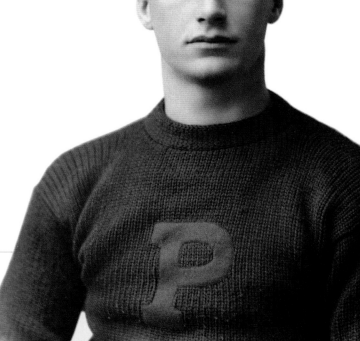

Robert Garrett 1897

and two gold medals. Garrett later served as a trustee for 40 years and president of his class for 64 years, and donated the Garrett Collection of Near Eastern Manuscripts.

Hobart Amory Hare (Hobey) Baker was generally regarded in his day as the greatest ice hockey player North America had yet produced. He was also an all-American football halfback. A fighter squadron commander in World War I, he crashed and died on a test flight in France with his orders home already in his pocket.

Emily Goodfellow, winner of 12 varsity letters in three sports, was one of Princeton's most versatile athletes ever. She played field hockey and lacrosse, and ranked second in the nation in squash.

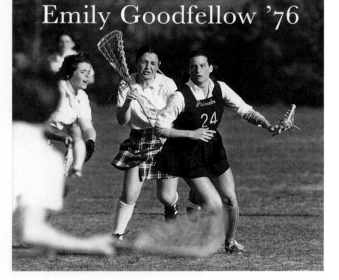

Emily Goodfellow '76

Hobey Baker '14

192

The Famous Poe Brothers

Of the six Poe brothers from Baltimore, three became all-Americans. Pictured are (l-r): Arthur Poe '00, Samuel Johnson Poe 1884, Neilson Poe 1897, Edgar Allan Poe 1891, Gresham Poe '02 and John Prentiss Poe, Jr. 1895. During the 1889 Harvard game, a Princeton alumnus was asked if Edgar was related to the great Edgar Allan Poe. "He is the great Edgar Allan Poe!" came the reply.

Holder of 25 Princeton basketball records, Bill Bradley is the only Tiger to score 40 or more points in a game, a feat he accomplished 11 times. His highest score, 58 points, came in Princeton's defeat of Wichita State to finish third in the 1965 NCAA finals. Also Princeton's career leader in rebounds, Bradley captained the U.S. Olympic team that won a gold medal in 1964. After a Rhodes Scholarship and a professional basketball career, he was elected a U.S. Senator in 1978.

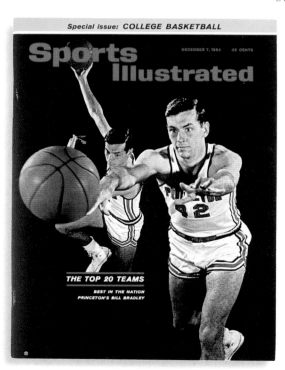

Tailback Dick Kazmaier led the Princeton football team to undefeated seasons in 1950 and 1951. The only Princeton player to win the Heisman Trophy as national player of the year, he won as a senior by the largest margin ever to that date.

Dick
Kazmaier
'52

Bill Bradley '65

Princeton Athletes

193

11

The Campus in Crisis

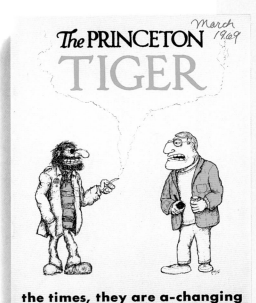

The PRINCETON *March 1969*
TIGER

the times, they are a-changing

Protests and demonstrations had been a familiar part of Princeton student life since its early years, but in the late 1960s and early 1970s they became intense, widespread and highly politicized as the war in Vietnam posed a crisis for college-age students and for American society. At Princeton, as at many other campuses, protests spread beyond the war to a variety of other issues: racism, poverty and lack of student participation in university decision making.

At Columbia, Berkeley, Kent State and elsewhere, unchecked passions and occasional violence wreaked havoc on student-faculty-administration relationships. Princeton, though severely tested by the turbulence of the times, managed to avoid the worst of the troubles. Extensive traditions, a strong culture and high self-esteem helped the university, even though this new era coincided with a sharp increase in diversity of all sorts, making Princeton less homogeneous than it had been before. The university's small size and residential character forced antagonists in the dramatic events to deal with one another as individuals. A radical student organizer commented, "It's too close a community—throw a brick and someone will recognize you."

Willingness to listen and an unprecedented degree of flexibility on the part of the university president and his administration, the trustees and faculty were crucial. In the end students themselves channeled the intense protests of the Age of Aquarius away from the destructiveness that afflicted many other campuses.

❦

In September 1965, greeting the incoming Class of 1969 in Alexander Hall, President Goheen was unconcerned about the problem of student protests, saying, "Only through disturbance comes growth. I would be worried if you were not disturbed."

S*trike T-shirt from May 1970.*

Meeting the trustees in the Faculty Room of Nassau Hall the following month, the president noted a growing student activism: "Partly this reflects normal youthful delight in kicking age and authority in the shins, but partly also perhaps it represents a deliberate effort to try to assert a greater role for students in the direction and management of the university, reflecting a nation-wide condition." If there was alienation at Princeton, he added, it probably was felt by only a tiny group, with 95 percent

or more of the students feeling no alienation at all.

Goheen's analysis did not reckon with the sharp escalation of the war in Vietnam, ordered by President Johnson in mid-1965 but presented as only an incremental change at the time. The fall of 1965 saw the founding of the local chapter of Students for a Democratic Society (SDS), which was the lead organization for radical campus activism. In November 30 undergraduates, 40 graduate students and 100 townspeople traveled to Washington to join the "March on Washington to End the War in Vietnam." The students won cheers and applause from fellow marchers by carrying a 10-foot-long orange and black banner blazoned with the simple but powerful message, "EVEN PRINCETON."

When President Johnson came to the campus in May 1966 to dedicate the new building of the Woodrow Wilson School of Public and International Affairs, he was peacefully picketed by a well-dressed, orderly group of close to 400 people, mostly students. SDS activists were surprised at the broad base

*U*nited States President Lyndon B. Johnson, escorted by Princeton President Robert Goheen, arrives for the dedication of the new Woodrow Wilson School building (now Robertson Hall) in May 1966.

*T*he EVEN PRINCETON banner, shown here at the May 2, 1968, Nassau Hall rally, indicated that anti-Vietnam war sentiment was strong even at a university that many considered a bastion of political conservatism.

(Continued on page six)

Photo by Bob Pariser

In the aftermath of Columbia, Princeton students marched on Nassau Hall May 2, 1968, calling for restructure

of support, symbolized by the fact that the organizational meeting of the SDS-led Princeton Ad Hoc Committee for an End to Intervention in Vietnam was held in Ivy Club, Prospect Avenue's oldest and most elitist. The *New York Times* gave the protest front-page coverage, catapulting SDS to new prominence on campus. In April 1967 SDS sponsored a dramatic full-page ad in the *Prince*. Under the headline "We Won't Go!" were the names of 66 students who pledged that "under no circumstances will we fight in Vietnam or surrender our opposition to this war."

In October 1967 SDS organized and led Princeton's first disruptive political protest—a sit-in at the Princeton branch of the Institute for Defense Analyses (IDA), a nonprofit corporation formed by a consortium of universities to do research for the Pentagon. IDA's Communications Research Division was headquartered in a building leased from the university on university-owned land located behind the Engineering Quadrangle at the east edge of the campus. The university argued that IDA was legally an off-campus facility and any trouble that might occur there was not its responsibility, but a matter for local police. Thirty students were arrested at the sit-in, most of whom went

A triptych of arrests from the IDA sit-in of October 1967.

On May 11, 1967, Alabama Governor George Wallace spoke to a largely hostile capacity crowd at Dillon Gymnasium. The building was surrounded by state police, and attendees were frisked as they entered the lobby. Some shouted "Sieg Heil!" as Wallace rose to speak. The Association of Black Collegians quietly and pointedly walked out.

limp and had to be dragged or thrown into police vehicles. Goheen, a hands-on president who was always present at moments of trouble, remarked, "This isn't Princeton," a much-quoted statement that was interpreted as an expression of shock at the sit-in. Goheen recalls that he actually intended only to point out that the property was not under university control.

Even while campus strife was growing rapidly, there were clear signs that Princeton's traditional conservatism was not dead. The same month as the first IDA sit-in in 1967, a poll of 1,800 students reported that 54 percent believed U.S. involvement in Vietnam was justified. Five hundred students said the bombing of North Vietnam should be stepped up. When Princeton SDS sponsored a regional conference on the campus for activists from the New York-New Jersey area the following month, the talk in the meetings was of revolutionary action. Nonetheless, Dotson Rader, a writer who covered the sessions for the *New Republic*, reported that during a luncheon break, "I wandered around the campus and heard the band play for the Princeton-Yale game and saw the students with their dates wander toward the stadium—as if no war were being fought and no people were in prison for opposing it, as if Harlem and Watts and the Mississippi Delta country did not exist, as if the world were just and men did not die senselessly."

As the news from Asia and urban America became bleaker, more students became engaged. In April 1968, after the Tet Offensive in Vietnam and the assassination of the Reverend Martin Luther King, Jr., in Memphis, the "On the Campus" columnist of the *Alumni Weekly*, John V. H. Dippel '68, wrote that "Princeton is no longer a four-year escape from contemporaneity, rather Princetonians thirst after current events; Huntley-Brinkley has replaced the leisurely pool game after dinner; the *New York Times* is standard equipment at the breakfast table. The quiet con-

Tight-lipped and grim-faced, Marion Sleet '69 takes part in a silent vigil at Palmer Square after the 1968 assassination of Dr. Martin Luther King, Jr.

templative scholar has all but vanished: Princeton has a foot in Vietnam, in New York City, in Memphis...."

Realizing that radical protest appealed to only a minority, although a growing and increasingly vocal one, SDS leaders at Princeton were more cautious than at many other campuses. "We try to speak primarily to the 500 or so who are liberals," said Richard Fried '68, an SDS leader, in an interview in his senior year. "But we have to walk a narrow line between working with and convincing these liberals to our way of thinking, and not going so far that we produce a conservative reaction."

At the May 2, 1968, rally, SDS member and Undergraduate Assembly President Peter Kaminsky '69 spoke from the steps of Nassau Hall not only to a massed crowd of students, faculty and staff (opposite), but also to the national press.

While the war in Southeast Asia was the central issue, protests on the Princeton campus were directed at a variety of causes. A high point of the 1968 demonstrations came on May 2 when more than 1,000 students and some faculty and staff gathered at Nassau Hall for an SDS-sponsored rally. As students sat to listen on the grassy lawn, the organizers presented a variety of demands, including the cutting of ties with the Institute for Defense Analyses, divestment of university investments in companies doing business in South Africa, more draft counseling and abolition of parietal restrictions on the hours of female visitors in dormitories. In response, Goheen announced his

Trustee Harold Helm '20 talks with a student.

Stan Kelley

ADVOCATE AND ARCHITECT OF
CONSTRUCTIVE CHANGE

More than 2,500 students and faculty assembled hastily in the Chapel on the night of April 30, 1970, within an hour after President Richard Nixon announced that, rather than winding down the war in Vietnam, the United States was invading Cambodia. Speakers expressed anger and frustration, and then Politics Professor Stanley Kelley, Jr., issued a stirring appeal to channel anger into constructive action for change. After Kelley spoke, the Chapel had to be evacuated because of a bomb threat.

support for "a fresh and searching review of the decision-making processes of the university." His declaration grew into the student-faculty-administration Committee on the Structure of the University under the leadership of politics professor Stanley Kelley, Jr., which advocated and achieved a greater student voice in governance, largely through a Council of the Princeton University Community (CPUC). Composed of students, faculty, staff and alumni, the council would meet monthly during the academic year, and its committees would, among other things, advise on the university's annual budget (Priorities Committee), develop rules of conduct on campus (Rights and Rules), consider stockholder questions (Resources) and assist in honorary degree selection (Governance).

Within weeks of the May rally, the *Daily Princetonian* reported that Princeton was on the verge of becoming a coeducational institution—the most fundamental change in undergraduate life in the university's history. By the end of the year, the trustees had abolished the contentious parietal rules, allocated funds for a new draft-counseling program and made public the Patterson report advocating the admission of at least 1,000 women undergraduates. Taking its cue from Goheen's declaration to the May 2 rally that "over the years, Princeton has changed in many ways and repeatedly shown its ability to adapt itself successfully to changing conditions," the university was in the process of extensive change, initiated from the top with prodding from below. The opening number of the 1969 Triangle show, reflecting the mood of the times, proclaimed:

A different kick—another way.

We just can't stick—to yesterday.

With many campus demands being satisfied, the protest movement at Princeton increasingly centered on the twin issues of racism and the Vietnam war. In March 1969 51 black students of the Association of Black Collegians (ABC) occupied New South administration building for 11 hours in a protest aimed at divestment of university investments in firms doing business in South Africa. Members of the mostly white SDS, whose popularity on campus had declined due to splits within the movement and increasingly radical tactics, sought unsuccessfully to join the protest but were allowed to take refuge in the building from the extremely cold weather for about three hours.

*F*ar removed from the strife on campus, astronaut Charles (Pete) Conrad, Jr., '53 became the third man to walk on the moon when his Apollo XII Intrepid landed on November 18, 1969. Conrad carried five Princeton flags. He presented one to the university, but it was destroyed by fire when it was sent to be framed. Pictured is the flag he presented to Colonial Club.

In the spring of 1970 President Nixon's forceful policies in Indochina, even while reducing the number of U.S. troops deployed in Asia, generated extensive antiwar protests on many U.S. campuses. On March 5 about 75 antiwar hecklers, some wearing red smears on their foreheads and Indian-style headbands, disrupted a speech to an ecology conference in Jadwin Gym by Secretary of the Interior Walter J. Hickel. "Talk about the war!" shouted some protesters, while others chanted, "Today's pigs, tomorrow's bacon! Nixon and Hickel better start shakin'!"

Goheen, who was sitting on the dais with Hickel, tried without success to quiet the disruption and warned that this violation of university rules on freedom of speech

The disruption of Secretary of the Interior Walter Hickel's speech on March 5, 1970, illustrated the escalating sense of student outrage that would reach a crescendo in May. This incident became widely known as the "Hickel Heckle."

would bring disciplinary action. Eventually charges were brought against 17 undergraduate and graduate students before the Judicial Committee of the newly created CPUC. After tumultuous public "trials," three students were suspended and nine others placed on probation. On the other side of the issue, more than 1,400 students and faculty members signed a letter of apology to Hickel. The interior secretary subsequently appealed to Nixon not to lose touch with campus sentiment; later that year he was fired from the cabinet.

The culmination of protest activity for the year and, as it turned out, the high point of demonstrations at Princeton came in reaction to President Nixon's announcement on April 30, 1970, that he had sent U.S. troops into Cambodia in what appeared to be a major widening of the war. Nixon's unexpected action shocked moderate and even normally conservative students and faculty members. Within days, more than half the colleges and universities in the country experienced protest demonstrations, involving close to 60 percent of the entire student population. Seventy-three campuses reported violent demonstrations, and at 26 schools the demonstrations involved serious clashes between students and police or military forces, including Kent State University in Ohio, where four students were killed, and Jackson State College in Mississippi, where two students were killed.

At Princeton about 2,500 people gathered in the University Chapel in an atmosphere of crisis within an hour after Nixon's announcement. In a passionately applauded speech, Sam Lipsman '71 declared, "When Dick Nixon moves into

President Goheen sat uncomfortably on stage behind Secretary Hickel. Goheen had shown both grace and wisdom in guiding the university through this turbulent era, but he was infuriated by the hecklers' display of rampant incivility. Below: Students traveled to Washington to present Secretary Hickel with a letter of apology bearing more than 1,400 signatures.

action, then it's time for Princeton University to get off its ass and move into action itself." In a sobering and effective speech, Professor Kelley appealed to the crowd to channel its anger into constructive action for change by working through the political system. This began a marathon series of debates

On May 6, 1970, angry students, some waving Vietcong flags, charged down Prospect Avenue to surround the Institute for Defense Analyses.

and discussions as students, faculty members and administrators met day after day in an atmosphere of high emotion.

There was widespread agreement at the outset that Princeton should "go on strike" rather than continue business as usual in this moment of crisis. According to the national press, Princeton became the first university in the nation to declare a strike. However, there was no consensus on the nature or objectives of the strike action. The turning point came at a mass meeting of nearly 4,000 students, faculty and staff members in Jadwin Gym on May 4. By a vote of 2,066 to 1,522, the meeting endorsed a "strike against the war" proposed by the Undergraduate Council that committed Princeton as an institution to work against expansion of the war, rather than a "strike against the university" proposed by more radical students.

Ten eating clubs canceled houseparties weekend for the first time since World War II, and many extracurricular activities were called off. Roughly 80 percent of students did not attend classes in the one remaining day of the spring semester. In a series of lengthy meetings, the faculty declared itself to be "outraged" by the expansion of the war and agreed to suspend final examinations for those who did not wish to take them. Meeting in emergency open session in Alexander Hall with Goheen presiding, the CPUC recommended a rearrangement of the fall academic calendar to permit a two-week recess immediately preceding the November elections during which students and faculty could work for political change. A local and eventually nationwide organization called the Movement for a New Congress was set up on the campus to encourage student participation in political action. These ideas became known nationally as the Princeton Plan and were adopted by many other universities.

Student advocates of direct action, primarily members of the various SDS factions, did not challenge the community-wide decisions head-on but aimed their militancy at the Institute for Defense Analyses on the edge of campus. Beginning on May 6, student demonstrators marched to IDA, chained the doors shut and began to paint the walls with graffiti. Police arrived to protect the building and IDA employees were sent home, but the students were permitted to continue their vigil. After five days of rising tension, IDA, armed with a court order, brought in police with riot helmets and night sticks to clear the area.

*T*he demonstrators stayed for five days in a siege that sometimes threatened to become lethally violent, much as the confrontations at Kent State and Jackson State just days earlier. When the students finally departed, the building was covered with graffitti and the grounds were littered with smoldering piles of trash.

After the police moved in, the protest took a violent turn when a fire was set in IDA's air-conditioning unit and a student was arrested for arson. About the same time, a small fire was discovered and put out in the basement of Nassau Hall. At the IDA building, in an ugly face-off, a hail of bottles was thrown at patrolling sheriff's deputies, who then produced and displayed their shotguns. "You could hear the click of their guns as they loaded the chambers," recalled Professor Aaron Lemonick *54, then dean of the graduate school and later dean of the faculty. Seeing a catastrophe in the making, Lemonick, Provost (later President) Bowen and Dean of Students Neil Rudenstine '56 (later President of Harvard University) persuaded the angry student demonstrators to back off. Within hours Goheen declared a state of emergency in the area of the university close to IDA, clearing it of all protesters. Simultaneously, Goheen was talking to the trustees about severing university ties to IDA. The demonstrations tapered off,

The commencement of 1970 was unlike any other in Princeton history. Because of the strike, seniors had not been required to take final course exams or senior comprehensives. Many were involved in political action, and there was a lingering tension in the air from the tumultuous events of the spring. Most seniors chose not to wear the traditional caps and gowns, feeling that "business as usual" was inappropriate. To add to the cacophony of the day, a plague of 17-year locusts (Magicicada septemdecem, right) had descended upon Princeton, creating a din that nearly drowned out the commencement speakers.

although IDA continued to be the subject of recurrent protests and arrests for two more years. It insisted on staying in the university-owned building until its lease ran out in 1975. Ironically, the building has since become the headquarters of the Center for Energy and Environmental Studies. Faint traces of the graffiti from the demonstrations more than two decades ago can still be seen.

Reviewing the developments at the end of 1970, the *Chronicle of Higher Education*, the leading professional journal in its field, reported that "students, faculty members, and administrators at Princeton seem to be moving together on political issues. Students' energies have been focused on the draft and Congress rather than on the institution itself, so that potential divisions between the campus constituents have been avoided." Antiwar protests recurred occasionally until American troops were out of Vietnam, and demonstrations and sit-ins continued into the 1990s on issues ranging from South African investments to staffing for sexual harassment counseling. In retrospect, however, the years of most serious crisis on the campus were over by the summer of 1970. Princeton had withstood and surmounted the worst of the storm.

*F*olk-rock icon Bob Dylan, who was awarded an honorary degree at the 1970 commencement, wrote a song about the experience entitled "Day of the Locust." To his right is Neil Rudenstine '56, then dean of students.

*B*reaking with tradition, the Class of 1970 requested that the FitzRandolph Gate be opened permanently to symbolize the university's interaction with its local community and the world beyond. Class President Stewart Dill led the class through the opened gate.

William G. Bowen, 1972-88

AS PRESIDENT, HE WAS RESPONSIBLE FOR
IMPLEMENTING COEDUCATION AND MANY
OTHER CHANGES THAT FLOWED FROM
THE TUMULTUOUS 1960S.

Although better known for his prowess at tennis and squash, Bill Bowen also could be found on the touch football fields. He was widely admired as an educator as well as a gifted administrator. When the Princeton University Press published his writings as president, the volume was titled, Ever the Teacher.

Born: Cincinnati, Ohio, 1933. B.A., Denison University, 1955. Ph.D. in Economics, Princeton, 1958.

Bill Bowen, as he was universally known, was provost of the university—in effect, chief of staff, deputy and heir-apparent to President Goheen—for four years before being selected to become Princeton's 17th president. Although there was a more extensive and more formal selection process than ever before, lasting eight months and involving faculty and student committees as well as trustees, it was clear from the first that Bowen was the odds-on favorite for the job.

As provost Bowen played an important role in the inception of coeducation. As president he was responsible for implementing it and many other changes that flowed from the tumultuous 1960s, including a more democratic and pervasive university governing process. Following the report of the Committee on Undergraduate Residential Life (CURL), which he convened, Bowen was responsible for creating the residential college system for all freshmen and sophomores.

During his tenure as president Bowen established seven new departments or programs and 46 new endowed professorships to strengthen the faculty. Five new buildings were built; a dozen others were expanded; and still others were renovated. He led the drive to establish the department of Molecular Biology and expanded Princeton's programs in a variety of other fields.

Asked about his most significant accomplishments as he announced his resignation in 1987, Bowen pointed first and foremost to his efforts to "reaffirm the mission of the place in a very fundamental sense, and by that I have in mind its independence, its openness to all points of view, its non-political character.... [This is] enormously important, more important perhaps than any of the tangibles that one might enumerate."

After retiring from Princeton, Bowen became president of the Andrew W. Mellon Foundation.

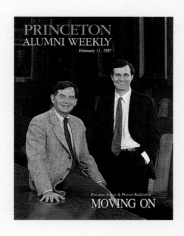

Two of Bowen's great partnerships at Princeton were with Neil Rudenstine '56, his provost for 10 years and later president of Harvard, and with his wife Mary Ellen, shown here in 1974 wearing part of the senior class's "Marxist" reunion costume.

12

New Realms
of Knowledge

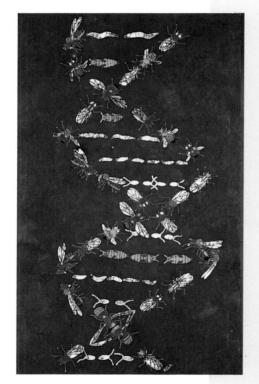

In the spring of 1953 two researchers at Cambridge University, James Watson and Francis Crick, deciphered the "double helix," the molecular structure of deoxyribonucleic acid (DNA), the substance that is the basis for the heredity of human beings and all other living things. Their discovery launched a dramatic new scientific epoch. Three decades later, in January 1983, Princeton's trustees met in a special session to consider what the university should do to bring itself abreast of the rapidly developing field of molecular biology.

The trustees had before them a 38-page confidential report by President Bowen, based on several years of exploration with the faculty and other outstanding scientists, on "Planning for the Future of Molecular Biology and the Life Sciences at Princeton." According to the report, "It is little exaggeration to say that this work—called biochemistry or molecular biology—is the most exciting and important scientific enterprise of the second half of the 20th century.... No great university can afford to fall behind in this critically important, growing edge of modern science."

In fact, Princeton had fallen behind, as Bowen's report candidly acknowledged. How it caught up and excelled is a vivid example of Princeton's determination and capacity to keep pace with changing intellectual and scientific currents and the proliferation of knowledge in the contemporary era. In the social sciences and humanities as well as science and engineering, Princeton's curriculum has changed with the times. In some respects it is notably different from the scholastic program in the immediate aftermath of World War II, to say nothing of the curricula of earlier decades and centuries.

❧

Serious work in biology has had a long history at Princeton, going back to Woodrow Wilson's recruitment of Edwin Grant Conklin as a biology professor in 1908 and the teaching of biochemical science beginning in 1920. Biochemistry became a department in 1970 as the field developed swiftly following the DNA discovery and other fundamental advances. However, Princeton did not adjust rapidly enough. Morale and recruitment lagged as the new department was squeezed between the older and stronger Chemistry and Biology departments, from which most of its personnel had originally been drawn.

Unable to compete effectively, Princeton's Biochemistry department had dwindled to three tenured professors by 1982. The number of professors in the overall field of the life sciences was a fraction of those blazing new trails at other universities. Bowen told the trustees in January 1983, "Our standing in many areas of the life sciences, which has never been

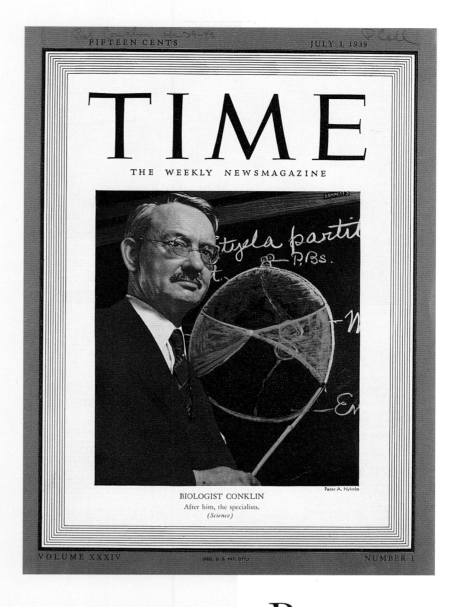

BIOLOGIST CONKLIN
After him, the specialists.
(Science)

Biologist Edwin Grant Conklin on the July 3, 1939, cover of Time Magazine.

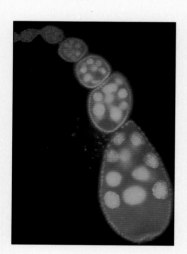

A string of Drosophila egg chambers stained with a blue dye to visualize the cell nuclei. The egg chamber contains 15 nurse cells and an oocyte which will develop into a mature fly egg.

Professors Arnold Levine (left) and Thomas Shenk in front of Lewis Thomas Laboratory, home of the department of Molecular Biology.

as high as it should have been, has fallen precipitously in recent years."

Because work in the life sciences typically involves group efforts in expensive facilities, Bowen recognized that "it will be possible to reverse our decline only by taking strong, even dramatic actions; half-measures are doomed to failure." His prescription was to recruit important new leadership and faculty and, at the same time, construct state-of-the-art laboratory facilities. It was a leap of faith, and a major gamble, to try to do both things at once. Bowen convinced the trustees, however, to seek $46 million for the faculty, staff and facilities of a new academic enterprise: a department of Molecular Biology.

By the time of the trustees' authorization, Bowen had found his future leaders: Arnold J. Levine, a former Princeton biochemist who had been lured away to the State University of New York at Stony Brook, and an eminent colleague there, Thomas E. Shenk. They were promptly appointed and began to scour the country for additional faculty. Within a year the university broke ground on the $29 million Lewis Thomas Laboratory that became the headquarters and flagship for the new department.

In 1994, after a decade of growth, the department headed by Levine was composed of 31 faculty members, 143 undergraduate majors, 104 graduate students, 115 postdoctoral associates and about 120 members of its technical and support staffs—more than 500 in all. Molecular Biology in 1994-95 was the fifth largest Princeton department, and first among science departments, in terms of the number of undergraduates choosing it as their area of concentration. Though still relatively small compared to life

School of Engineering

This tiny Princeton shield, approximately 300 millionths of a meter in width, was created by a chemical engineering group at Princeton. Composed of platinum thinly coated with titanium, it shows an uneven pattern of chemical waves during carbon monoxide oxidation.

Engineering at Princeton traces its origins to the benefactions of John Cleve Green (below), founder in 1872 of the School of Science, and to the pioneering efforts of two early professors in that school, Cyrus Fogg Brackett and Charles McMillan. McMillan came to Princeton in 1875 to fill a civil engineering chair that had been endowed that year by Green and to teach the college's first engineering course. He is shown above with his 1892 class. Under Brackett's leadership Princeton offered its first graduate-level engineering course, in electrical engineering, in 1889. In 1921 the university formed a School of Engineering with courses in civil, chemical, electrical, mechanical, and mining (later geological) engineering. During World War II the school added aeronautical engineering. A half-century later, the school's five departments were Chemical Engineering, Civil Engineering and Operations Research, Computer Science, Electrical Engineering, and Mechanical and Aerospace Engineering. In 1962 the school moved into the Engineering Quadrangle and was renamed the School of Engineering and Applied Science.

science organizations at many major universities, Princeton's department was considered among the nation's top 10 in quality—some say the top five—in a field that is still advancing at tremendous speed. Other aspects of biology are studied at Princeton in an excellent but separate and much smaller department of Ecology and Evolutionary Biology.

Another newly emerging field of knowledge, computer science, owes much of its early development to figures associated with Princeton, particularly the illustrious Professor John von Neumann and other mathematicians of the 1930s. While most of the early work underpinning the development of computer science at Princeton took place in the department of Mathematics, the center of gravity for computer research later moved to the School of Engineering and Applied Science and its department of Electrical Engineering, which in 1975 became the department of Electrical Engineering and Computer Science (EECS, popularly known as "eeeks").

As was the case in molecular biology, Princeton in the 1980s realized it had to make much greater efforts to keep pace

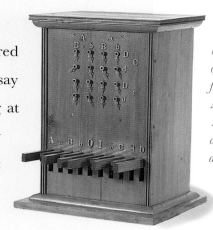

The Logic Machine, invented in the late 1870s by Allan Marquand, Class of 1874, was an ingenious forerunner of the computer. Marquand later founded Princeton's department of Art and Archaeology, to which he devoted his talent and wealth for over 40 years.

John von Neumann (right) and Institute for Advanced Study director Robert Oppenheimer in front of an early computer.

Graduate student Kyle Harms at the Mpala Research Center in Kenya. The center was established in 1992 with Princeton as one of five trustees. The department of Ecology and Evolutionary Biology uses the center for research and teaching in evolution, conservation, natural resource management and related disciplines of tropical biology.

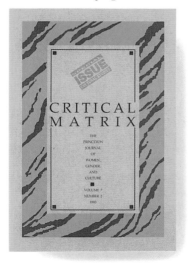

Anthropology Professor Kay Warren teaching the introductory course in the Women's Studies program in 1985, four years after the program's inception. Below: Critical Matrix: The Princeton Journal of Women, Gender and Culture, *founded in 1985, is published twice yearly by graduate students affiliated with the Women's Studies program.*

with this rapidly expanding field. After extensive research, including visits to well-established departments in several other universities, Princeton in 1985 divided EECS into two departments, Computer Science and Electrical Engineering. The old joint department was composed of 23 faculty members and offered 36 courses for undergraduates. In 1994-95 Computer Science alone had a faculty of 19 teaching 23 courses, while Electrical Engineering was composed of 26 faculty members teaching 34 courses. One indication of the scale of change is that two-thirds of the faculty members in the two departments had come to Princeton since the departments were divided less than a decade before.

In nearly every branch of scholarship, knowledge has grown exponentially since World War II, and Princeton's curriculum has expanded with it. Since my freshman year at Princeton, 1948-49, the number of academic departments has increased from 26 to 32, and the number of special interdisciplinary academic programs has skyrocketed from three to more than 30. Of the latter, 12 have been established in the past eight years: Applications of Computing, Applied and Computational Mathematics, Cognitive Studies, Engineering Biology, Environmental Studies, Hellenic Studies, Jewish Studies, Language and Culture, Materials Science and Engineering, Medieval Studies, Musical Performance, and Visual Arts. In addition, undergraduates majoring in engineering may participate in topical programs in energy and environment, photonics, robotics and intelligent systems, and transportation.

The programs in Women's Studies, dating from 1981, and Afro-American Studies, which started earlier but was revitalized in 1985, had difficult birthing and growing pains. However, both eventually blossomed. When the Nobel prize in literature was awarded in 1993 to Chloe Anthony (Toni) Morrison, holder of the Robert F. Goheen Professorship in the Council of the Humanities, it gave international recognition not only to her but to the high standing of Princeton's Afro-American Studies and Creative Writing programs.

As these new interdisciplinary programs have emerged to bring diverse subjects into clearer focus, one of Princeton's premier interdisciplinary efforts continues to be its oldest: the Woodrow Wilson School of Public and International Affairs, founded in 1930, which has sought from its inception to integrate scholarship in economics, history, politics and allied subjects. The school's outstanding reputation and its unique program, including its policy conferences on current issues for undergraduates, have been a magnetic attraction for many prospective students, including the author

*W*ilson Hall (top) was built in 1951. On May 20, 1963, it was jacked up onto 12 steel tracks and moved from Washington Road to its present site, where it was renamed Corwin Hall. A new building, designed by Minuro Yamasaki and now known as Robertson Hall, was erected in its place to house the expanding Woodrow Wilson School of Public and International Affairs.

Evolution of Academic Departments

Between 1948-49 and 1994-95, the number of academic departments at Princeton increased from 26 to 32. At the same time, the number of interdisciplinary programs increased from three to more than 30.

1 9 4 8   1 9 9 5

Humanities

1948	1995
Art and Archaeology	Art and Archaeology
	Architecture, School of
Classics	Classics
English	English
Modern Languages and Literatures	Germanic Languages and Literatures
	Romance Languages and Literatures
	Slavic Languages and Literatures
Music	Music
Oriental Studies	East Asian Studies
	Near Eastern Studies
Philosophy	Philosophy
Religion	Religion
	Comparative Literature

Social Sciences

1948	1995
Economics and Social Institutions	Anthropology
	Economics
	Sociology
History	History
Politics	Politics
Woodrow Wilson School	Woodrow Wilson School

Natural Sciences

1948	1995
Astronomy	Astrophysical Sciences
Biology	Ecology and Evolutionary Biology
	Molecular Biology
Chemistry	Chemistry
Geology	Geological and Geophysical Sciences
Mathematics	Mathematics
Physics	Physics
Psychology	Psychology

Engineering and Applied Science

1948	1995
Aeronautical	Mechanical and Aerospace Engineering
Mechanical	
Chemical	Chemical Engineering
Civil	Civil Engineering and Operations Research
Geological	
Basic	
Electrical	Electrical Engineering
	Computer Science

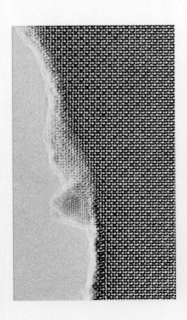

The field-emission-gun ultrahigh resolution transmission electron microscope at the Princeton Materials Institute can photograph materials at their atomic level. In this sample of perovskite ($CaFeTi_2O_6$), the space filled by individual atoms is clearly visible. Each space is approximately three ten-billionths of a meter in diameter.

of this book, and have substantially strengthened the university's faculty in the social sciences.

Shifts in departmental structures and the addition of special interdisciplinary programs do not begin to describe  the extent of change in the undergraduate curriculum due to the expansion of knowledge, the broadening of interests and the emergence of important new tools for scholarly analysis.

The department of Economics and Social Institutions that I knew as a freshman subsequently divided into three departments: Anthropology, Economics and Sociology. There were 19 courses on economic topics in the department in 1948-49. By 1994-95 the Economics department was offering 30 courses. Amid staples such as courses on the national economy and money and banking were two courses each in macroeconomics and microeconomics and three in econometrics. The department was also teaching courses in urban economics, the economics of uncertainty, development economics, international monetary economics, and even Soviet-type economics and the Chinese economy.

My long-standing personal and professional interest in East Asia was kindled by Princeton's only social science course in the field at the time, Professor William Lockwood's Politics 314, which dealt with the political and social development of China and Japan. I also took Chinese art and could have taken some of the four courses given then in elementary and intermediate Chinese.

In 1994-95 the department of East Asian Studies—which along with Near Eastern Studies was carved out of the old department of Oriental Languages and Literatures—offered 55 courses, including 20 courses of Chinese language instruction or readings in Chinese as well as 14 courses in Japanese language and four courses in Korean (neither of which was taught at Princeton in my day) and 15 courses in East Asian literature and civilization. The undergraduate catalog also listed 17 additional courses on East Asian topics in other departments: three in Art and Archaeology, one in Economics, four in History, one in Music, one in Politics, four in Religion and three in Sociology.

In many areas the content of courses has also changed tremendously. General Astronomy, the introductory course in the department of Astronomy in 1948, covered "our present general knowledge of

the earth, moon, sun, planets, comets and meteors, and of the stars, the galaxy and the nebulae; and the methods by which this knowledge has been attained." The introductory course of the current department of Astrophysical Sciences (renamed in 1962 when its scope was enlarged) adds to the earlier list of topics "quasars, black holes, cosmology and life in the universe." Undergraduate majors are also offered courses in the structure of stars and in interstellar matter and star formation and are expected to take courses in physics covering "mechanics, electromagnetic theory, optics, thermodynamics, kinetic theory and atomic physics."

P*rofessor John McPhee '53 in his East Pyne office in 1985.*

Another striking change is the elaboration of courses in the creative arts. The old Creative Arts program of my undergraduate era offered a single course in creative writing under a distinguished resident fellow or faculty member and "open ateliers" in sculpture and painting. Today's Creative Writing program offers five courses under distinguished faculty, including Nobel prize winner Toni Morrison, novelists Joyce Carol Oates and Russell Banks, and nonfiction writer John McPhee '53, while the Visual Arts program offers 30 courses ranging from studio courses in drawing, painting, photography, sculpture and ceramics to special courses in the development of cinema and problems of film and video practice, and the program in Theater and Dance offers courses on acting, directing, playwriting and choreography. Supplementing these offerings are opportunities to work with the "fellows" brought to campus each year by the Council of the Humanities.

Just what future the Designer of the universe has provided for the souls of men I do not know, I cannot prove. But I find that the whole of Nature confirms my confidence that, if it is not like our noblest hopes and dreams, it will transcend them.

H E N R Y   N O R R I S

R U S S E L L   1 8 9 7

Russell graduated insigni cum laude (with extraordinary honor), a designation the faculty never used before or since.

In view of the fragmentation arising from the explosion of information and creativity, the broad survey courses introducing students to various departments and disciplines are more impor-

New Realms of Knowledge

tant than ever. They still exist at Princeton and are often taught by the most eminent scholars.

Through much of its history Princeton has emphasized the process of learning more than the acquisition of information as the most essential element of its academic enterprise. As early as 1752, Aaron Burr, Sr., its second president, wrote of the college's intention to proceed "not so much in the method of a dogmatic institution, by prolix discourses on the different branches of the sciences, by burdening the memory and infusing heavy and disagreeable tasks; as in the Socratic way of free dialogue between teacher and pupil, or between the students themselves, under the inspection of their tutors." Education by personal

Portrait of a painter in her studio, from the senior thesis of Visual Arts student Lori Hayes '95. Right: Student modern dance performance choreographed by students under the direction of Professor Ze'eva Cohen of the Theater and Dance program.

interaction was the crux of Woodrow Wilson's preceptorial system and of the independent research and writing that have been hallmarks of a Princeton education.

In the spring of 1993 these objectives were given formal recognition by the Strategic Planning Committee on Undergraduate Education, chaired by Dean of the College Nancy Weiss Malkiel and including undergraduates as well as faculty members. The committee began its work by formulating these ambitious goals for a Princeton undergraduate education:

- *the ability to think, speak and write clearly;*
- *the ability to reason critically and systematically;*
- *the ability to conceptualize and solve problems;*
- *the ability to think independently;*
- *the ability to take initiative and work independently;*
- *the ability to work in cooperation with others and learn collaboratively;*
- *the ability to judge what it means to understand something thoroughly;*
- *the ability to distinguish the important from the trivial, the enduring from the ephemeral;*
- *familiarity with different modes of thought (including quantitative, historical, scientific, moral and aesthetic);*
- *depth of knowledge in a particular field;*
- *the ability to see connections among disciplines, ideas and cultures;*
- *the ability to pursue lifelong learning.*

Although today's Princeton is many years away from the Princeton of Witherspoon and McCosh, it is likely that those great educators would have recognized these enduring concepts, even if they might have used different words to describe them. But there is no way they could have recognized their applications in the explorations of the mysteries of the cell, the science of computer logic or the diverse languages and cultures of East Asia.

Dean of the College Nancy Weiss Malkiel.

Nobel Prize Winners

WRITER
Guy Ellis

ARTIST
Lisa Bhajan

Sir W. Arthur Lewis,
*professor of economics and
international affairs at
Princeton from 1963 until his
death in 1991, specialized in
the economics of developing
countries. Among other positions, he served as vice chancellor of the University of the
West Indies and chancellor of
the University of Guyana.*

Physics

1927	Arthur H. Compton, Ph.D. 1916
1928	Owen W. Richardson, professor of physics
1933	P.A.M. Dirac, visiting lecturer, mathematics and physics
1937	Clinton J. Davisson, Ph.D. 1911
1945	Wolfgang Pauli, lecturer in physics
1956	John Bardeen, Ph.D. 1936
1961	Robert Hofstadter, Ph.D. 1938
1963	Eugene P. Wigner, Jones Professor of Mathematical Physics
1965	Richard P. Feynmann, Ph.D. 1942
1972	John Bardeen, Ph.D. 1936
1977	Philip W. Anderson, Ph.D. 1949, Joseph Henry Professor of Physics
1978	Arno A. Penzias, visiting lecturer with rank of professor
1979	Steven Weinberg, Ph.D. 1957
1980	Val L. Fitch, Cyrus Fogg Brackett Professor of Physics
1980	James W. Cronin, professor of physics
1993	Joseph H. Taylor, James S. McDonnell Distinguished University Professor of Physics
1993	Russell Hulse, principal research physicist, Princeton Plasma Physics Laboratory

Chemistry

1948	Arne Tiselius, post-doctoral fellow
1951	Edwin M. McMillan, Ph.D. 1933 (physics)

Economics

1979	Sir W. Arthur Lewis, James Madison Professor of Political Economy
1992	Gary S. Becker '51
1994	John F. Nash, Ph.D. 1950, senior research mathematician

Literature

1929	Thomas Mann, lecturer in the humanities
1936	Eugene O'Neill '10
1993	Toni Morrison, Robert F. Goheen Professor in the Humanities

Physiology and Medicine

1950	Edward C. Kendall, visiting professor of chemistry

Peace

1919	Woodrow Wilson 1879, member of the faculty and president of the university

Toni Morrison, author of Song of Solomon *(winner of the 1977 National Book Critics Circle Award),* Beloved *(winner of the 1988 Pulitzer prize) and other works, at the Nobel ceremonies and on a Swedish stamp.*

Since the Nobel prize was established in 1901, Princetonians have won at least once in each field. Princeton educated the only person ever to win two prizes in the same field: John Bardeen *36 (far right), Physics, in 1956 and 1972. Other double laureates, but in different fields, were Marie Curie (Physics 1903 and Chemistry 1911) and Linus Pauling (Chemistry 1954 and Peace 1962).

*Physics laureates Joseph Taylor (left), Philip Anderson *49 and Val Fitch standing with Antoine Pevsner's "Construction in the Third and Fourth Dimension" outside Jadwin Hall.*

13

The Rise of
the Residential
Colleges

From 1834 until 1846 the college refectory on William Street served as Princeton's first commons. It was inexpensive but spartan. Students dubbed it the "poor house," and most chose to eat at village boarding houses or to band together in informal eating clubs.

Since the days of Woodrow Wilson the questions of where and under what circumstances students should live, eat and party have been difficult ones for Princeton. Under Wilson's visionary quad plan, the housing, feeding and social life of all undergraduates would have been centered in a series of residential quadrangles. While a version of the plan was later adopted at Harvard and Yale, principally for upperclass students, its defeat at Princeton continued the fragmentation of nonacademic life.

For most of the 20th century, virtually all undergraduates lived in dormitory rooms unconnected to their dining facilities. Most freshmen and sophomores ate their meals in Commons, the five Gothic dining halls erected in the immediate post-Wilson era, and socialized in a variety of piecemeal and makeshift arrangements until joining Prospect Avenue clubs in the second semester of sophomore year. Juniors and seniors ate their meals and attended parties in the eating clubs, which, as private institutions, were a frequent source of tension with the university.

"*Watcha Waiter!*" *was the warning cry at the Madison Hall Commons with its long tables and busy student servers. These photos are from 1937 (opposite) and the early post–World War II era (below).*

There was no serious connection between any of these facilities and academic advising or the scholarly life of the university.

In the 1960s Commons became extremely crowded due to the gradual expansion of the undergraduate body. When enrollment jumped by another one-third in the 1970s because of coeducation, the old system for feeding freshmen and sopho-mores became inadequate, leading to a patchwork of supple-mental arrangements. At the same time, as costs increased and membership in the upperclass eating clubs declined, some clubs folded and others were going broke.

*T*his brownstone, later known as Ivy Hall, was constructed on Mercer Street to house Princeton's law school, which opened in 1847 and graduated a total of seven students, the last in 1852. Beginning in 1879 the building served as the first home of Ivy Club, Princeton's first eating club.

A collection of eating club ties from the March 1927 issue of Tiger Magazine.

In the late 1970s President Bowen established a Committee on Undergraduate Residential Life, known by its acronym CURL, to reconsider Princeton's dining and social options. The result was a recommendation to the trustees in May 1979 to establish five residential colleges to house, feed and provide social facilities for all freshmen and sophomores. With surprising speed, the funds were raised, making possible by the mid-1980s the most important change in undergraduate living arrangements of the century. Meanwhile, a university offer, arising from CURL, to underwrite the eating clubs was rejected by the clubs after extensive debate.

❦

The five vaulted Gothic dining halls of Commons—Madison, Upper and Lower Cloister, Upper and Sub Eagle—were places of bustle and clatter at mealtime from their dedication in 1916. Although complaints about the fare in Commons were a constant refrain in student life, virtually all freshmen and sophomores shared the same dining experience around the long tables of these halls. "The evils of a separate club system such as exists in Princeton only during the junior and senior years are to a large extent mitigated by the close and general associations formed during the years in Commons," wrote Henry T. Dunn '17 in the *Alumni Weekly* in the first year of the new buildings.

By the 1970s Princeton had outgrown the Commons system under the pressure of increasing crowding and student demands for more eating and social options. The first experimental residential

college, named for Woodrow Wilson, was inaugurated in 1968, with membership open to all four classes. Students lived in the dormitories of the "Old New Quad" (1915, 1922, 1937, 1938, 1939 and Dodge-Osborn halls) and took their meals at Wilcox Hall, which had been serving as the dining and social center for a more loosely organized group of students known as the Woodrow Wilson Society. Two years later the converted Princeton Inn became a second residential college following the admission of women. Two defunct eating clubs on Prospect Avenue were purchased by the university to become Adlai Stevenson Hall, a social and dining complex that opened in 1969, and other university-sponsored dining options were established in the 1970s, including the Madison Society, whose members ate breakfast in Wilcox Hall, lunch at the student center and dinner on the seventh floor of the New South administration building. In 1971-72 about 1,300 students ate in Commons, about 900 ate in Prospect Avenue eating clubs, about 1,200 took their meals in university-sponsored residential colleges and halls, about 420 "independents" made their own arrangements using dormitory kitchens or eating in town, and the rest lived off campus. In 1973 the university constructed Spelman Halls, an eight-building complex that provided apartment-style units, including kitchens, for 220 students.

Undergraduates and friends play a game of blow pong at Tower Club in 1969.

Bicker cartoon from the *February 4, 1972, issue of the* Daily Princetonian.

The worsening straits of the eating clubs led to the closing of some clubs and a decision by others to abandon selectivity and become open to all upperclass students on a sign-in basis. By 1978 there were eight open clubs and five selective clubs. The age-old controversy about the club system continued, as demonstrated by a chanting crowd of more than 300 students who marched up and down Prospect Avenue in February 1978 carrying lighted candles and banners reading, "Options yes, Bicker no! Prospect Street has to go!" The march organizer, Robert K. Massie '78, told the *Daily Princetonian* that the fundamental source of Princeton's social problems was "the contradiction between its attempt to attract students of diverse backgrounds while failing to provide a proper social environment." Later that month Bowen

Robert Massie '78 *spoke at an anti-bicker rally on the steps of Robertson Hall in February 1978.*

appointed the CURL committee to explore new social and dining arrangements and their potential impact on the quality of undergraduate life.

Bowen recalled that "a mix of principle and practicality" led CURL to recommend creating five residential colleges involving all members of the freshman and sophomore classes, while proposing to prop up the remaining eating clubs for upperclass students. "The principle was that students need most the benefits of a college system when they first come.... [With] much bigger entering classes, a lot of people were just getting lost," according to Bowen. The practical side, he said, was that the university could hardly afford to duplicate the existing eating and social facilities on Prospect Avenue.

As the committee studied the possibilities, according to Professor Joan S. Girgus, who was then dean of the college and a leading member of CURL, it did not take long to see the benefits of creating five units of manageable size that would integrate dining and social life with academic life more extensively than ever before. "We wanted students to be able to see these [parts of their lives] as more of a piece," Girgus said.

At the time of the May 1979 CURL report and the trustees' October 1979 endorsement, it was far from certain that the residential college system, which had been under discussion periodically since Wilson's abortive quad plan, would come to fruition. At best it was widely expected that many years would be required to raise the millions of dollars needed. Surprisingly, nearly all the money was raised within a year, and creation of the three new colleges began shortly after that.

"As with coeducation, once the decision had been made to go, it was critical to move as fast as we could," Bowen recalled. As often before in Princeton's history, prominent alumni were the key. Acting on a tip, Bowen invited former trustee Lee D. Butler

The Five Residential College Emblems

BUTLER

FORBES

MATHEY

ROCKEFELLER

WILSON

Exercise room at Mathey
College. Below: 1944 watercolor of Joline and Campbell
dormitories, now part of
Mathey College.

'22 to Princeton in late December 1979 to discuss the plans
for the first new residential college, which was to be established
in the existing cluster of dormitories (then known as the
"New New Quad") just south of the existing Wilson College.
Butler had transferred to Princeton in his sophomore year and
worked his way through college, with little time or inclination
for Prospect Avenue social life. He stayed on to earn his
M.A. in history, marry Margaret Burchard Fine, who came
from a distinguished Princeton University family, and operate
an automobile sales agency in Princeton before moving to
Washington, D.C., to become a highly successful automobile
dealer and civic leader.

Watercolor of Walker
(left), Feinberg and 1937 dormitories. Feinberg, 1937 and
parts of Walker house students
in Wilson College.

In conversation with Butler, university Secretary Thomas H. Wright, Jr., '62 said that "residential/social life has been the weak side of Princeton for 80 years" and that this was a historic chance to create a new balance. This resonated strongly with Butler, who decided, with his wife, to donate to the university the 5,000-acre farm on which they lived in Virginia's hunt country. Princeton sold the property for more than $3 million to renovate and endow the new college, which subsequently was named for Butler.

Butler's gift opened a funding floodgate. In April 1980 trustee Laurance S. Rockefeller '32 gave $5 million, later augmented by $1.5 million more from the Rockefeller family, to redevelop the northwestern corner of the campus, including part of the former Commons, as Rockefeller College in commemoration of his brother, the late John D. Rockefeller III '29. In September the Bunbury Foundation of Morristown, New Jersey, contributed $1.75 million in memory of its founder, longtime trustee Dean Mathey '12, to support the third new institution, also in the vicinity of Commons, which became Mathey College.

Holiday tree-trimming
party in Mathey College.

G*ordon Wu Hall (top), the social and dining facility for Butler College, was designed by architect Robert Venturi '47. Venturi points out details in the newly remodeled Forbes College to Malcolm Forbes '41 (left) and Malcolm Forbes, Jr. '70. Venturi's wife and architect partner Denise Scott Brown is in the center. Venturi's sketch (right) of the entrance to Wu Hall appeared on the September 1983 cover of Architectural Record.*

In the meantime Bowen flew to Hong Kong and persuaded Gordon Wu '58 to contribute the $3.5 million required to build the social and dining center that was needed for the new Butler College. It was eventually named Wu Hall and is the only building on campus identified with Chinese characters. The three new colleges, together with improvements to the existing Wilson College, left the renovation and endowment of Princeton Inn College as the only major piece of the five-college plan yet to be financed. During a break in a board of trustees meeting in the fall of 1983, at a time when the new colleges were being opened and dedicated one after another, trustee Malcolm Forbes '41, chairman and editor-in-chief of *Forbes Magazine*, asked Bowen to walk with him over to Princeton Inn. "What would it cost to fix this up properly?" the publisher asked. About $3 million, the president replied.

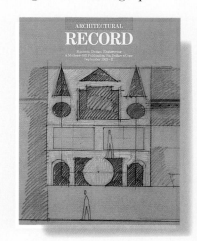

"Done," said Forbes, adding that "the counters in the counting house will just have a little less to count now." Forbes College, named in honor of Malcolm Forbes' eldest son, Steve '70, was dedicated in November 1984.

Once the new residential colleges were up and running, they had a major impact on the lives of freshmen and sophomores, who are assigned randomly to one of the five colleges during initial registration. Each college has a senior faculty member who serves as college master, a director of studies who is responsible for academic advising and disciplinary matters, and several dozen other faculty members, administrators and other members of the Princeton academic community as fellows. This staffing "sends a clear signal that they are to be centers not only for living but for learning," a university report declared in 1994. In addition, each college sponsors a variety of social, sports and recreational activities for its members. In 1986 the faculty inaugurated a program of one-semester freshman seminars in the residential colleges on subjects of the faculty members' own devising, which ranged in 1994-95 from the Cold War to Viruses to Freud's Writings on Politics, Culture and Religion. The highly successful seminars have increased to 45 per year and are to be expanded further.

An advertisement for the Princeton Inn (now Forbes College) that appeared in the 1937 issue of the Bric-a-Brac.

The CURL recommendations regarding the Prospect Avenue eating clubs generated most of the controversy that swirled around the report and touched off two years of intense negotiations between the university administration and the clubs. CURL proposed to underwrite the existing clubs by guaranteeing an adequate level of membership by juniors and seniors, most of whom would be required to have board contracts with the

university or with a participating club, and by supporting expensive maintenance, which in many cases had been long deferred. In return, participating clubs would have to guarantee that membership would be available to all students on the basis of open admissions.

When the five selective clubs opted out of the arrangement, the university concluded it would have to win support of at least seven of the eight nonselective or open clubs to make the plan viable. But after intense debate, Campus, Cloister and finally Quadrangle voted not to join, which killed the proposal.

In February 1979, in the midst of the CURL discussions, Sally Frank '80 filed a discrimination complaint with the New Jersey Division on Civil Rights against the three remaining all-male eating clubs, Tiger Inn, Ivy and Cottage. The agency initially turned down the complaint on the grounds that the clubs were private organizations, but it reversed itself in 1983 after Frank persisted. In the course of a legal battle that went up to the New Jersey Supreme Court, all three clubs eventually opened their memberships to women. Although strongly criticized by some students and alumni, Frank was praised by others. In June 1990 the Alumni Council bestowed on Frank its annual Award for Service to Princeton, citing her as "a loving critic" of the university.

In addition to the colleges and clubs, Princeton offers an astonishing array of extracurricular activities that are central to undergraduate life, most of them at the initiative of students. As of the 1994-95 school year, 166 student organizations,

plus the Undergraduate Student Government and the officers of the four undergraduate classes, were officially recognized by the dean of student life. (The largest organization, the Student Volunteers Council, engaged more than 900 students a week in various community service activities.) In addition, nearly 1,800 students, about 40 percent of the undergraduate body, participated in intercollegiate sports on more than 60 teams and crews at either the varsity or club level. The university estimated that nearly 65 percent of all undergraduates and 600 teams played in the intramural program.

The first snowfall of winter brings the Nude Olympics to Rockefeller College. Sophomore class participants gather in Holder courtyard, perform calisthenics, then run en masse through campus.

The cloisters of Holder courtyard at dusk.

Harold T. Shapiro, 1988-

Harold and Vivian Shapiro carried lacrosse sticks to lead the 1994 P-rade after Princeton's men's and women's teams both won their national titles.

An alumnus of the graduate school with a 1964 Ph.D. in economics, Shapiro returned as Princeton's 18th president in 1988 after 24 years at the University of Michigan, including eight as its president.

246

Born: Montreal, Canada, 1935. B-Comm., McGill University, 1956. Ph.D. in Economics, Princeton, 1964.

Harold Shapiro graduated from Montreal's McGill University with the highest academic honor of its Faculty of Commerce, the Lieutenant Governor's Medal. After five years in business, he enrolled in graduate school at Princeton. He earned his Ph.D. in three years and then joined the faculty of the University of Michigan, where he served for 24 years as professor of economics and public policy and as president from 1980 to 1988.

On January 8, 1988, he was installed as Princeton's 18th president; he also holds an appointment as professor of economics and public affairs. Despite the pressures of office, he has taught sections of Economics 101, a graduate seminar in health policy and freshman seminars on the history of higher education. His accomplishments as president have included creation of a Center for Human Values and new institutes in materials science and the environment, as well as efforts to increase the participation of women and representatives of minority groups in all aspects of university life.

In 1993 he published a strategic planning document, "Princeton University: Continuing to Look Ahead," that was widely distributed on campus and mailed to all alumni. He concluded that document by describing the mid-1990s as a time of "three C's: celebration, commitment, and challenge. We have every right to celebrate all that Princeton has accomplished over its 250 years; we remain strongly committed to its fundamental characteristics and aspirations; and we face the continuing challenges of educational and scholarly excellence, of service..., and of leadership...."

A prominent and highly respected national spokesman for higher education and research, Shapiro has chaired several national associations of university presidents and a number of important government or government/university committees.

*A*fter Shapiro's installation, the entire university community was invited to a reception in Jadwin Gymnasium. Among those attending was his grandson, Joey Kabourek.

*F*rom 1990 to 1992 Shapiro served on President George Bush's Council of Advisors on Science and Technology. He was vice chairman of a council panel that produced a major report in December 1992 on research-intensive universities and the nation.

14

Into the Future

M *arble tiger flanking the Ferris Thompson Gateway in front of Bowen Hall on Prospect Avenue.*

A lmost everyone who has known Princeton University well over a long period of years has been struck at one time or another by a notable paradox. On the one hand, the university has experienced great change physically, academically, in the diversity, interests and activities of its student body and faculty, and in many other ways, as the words and pictures on these pages testify. At the same time, Princeton seems to have changed little in its fundamental character, in the culture of the place.

From its earliest beginnings Princeton centered its aspirations and energies on undergraduate teaching. To a greater extent than at other schools of its size and caliber, this remained its central objective even after the transformation of scholarship that created the great American research universities of this century. Perhaps because of Princeton's physical characteristics and location—a residential university of great beauty, conveniently situated in a nonurban setting between New York and Philadelphia—it has been able to attract a succession of exceptional scholar-teachers without the allure, or the distraction, of separate professional schools of law, medicine, business administration or other disciplines. In the words of a distinguished early 20th-century dean of the faculty, Robert K. Root, Princeton has "maintained its character as a university without losing the character of a college."

What, then, about the future? After celebrating 250 years of its history, from the tiny beginnings in a parsonage in Elizabeth, New Jersey, through the move to Princeton and the great events of succeeding centuries, where does Princeton University go from here?

❧

In search of answers, I called on President Shapiro in his office at One Nassau Hall late one afternoon. Sitting at his desk in the historic old building, flanked by a computer terminal and a television set while a fax machine on a table behind him spewed out information from a distant city, Shapiro addressed both continuity and change.

"I do not believe we are going through a period now where we are going to see heroic or radical changes in what Princeton will be," he began. Despite the new communications technology that has wired up the campus and the world outside, Shapiro said he did not envisage the residential community of students and scholars being replaced by dispersed Princetonians "hanging out at the Internet." Intellectual growth and personal growth interact and are intertwined like twisted pairs of wires, he observed, and the residential setting and hands-on method of instruction will not be replaced in the foreseeable future.

L antern on the south side of Firestone Library, with the Dulles reading room beyond.

"What I do believe, however, is that if Princeton is going to maintain its position of leadership in higher education, it has to define for itself and execute a program which is in some sense unique, in the sense that no one will be able to copy us. People may copy parts of what we do, but they will not be able to become us," the president said. And the essence of Princeton's uniqueness, flowing out of its past and present, is to be "the outstanding place anywhere for education" and at the same time remain "a world-class center of scholarship." In this pursuit, he continued, "I see Princeton as exploring a well-understood path" of combining excellence in both teaching and scholarship "but in a new era that is going to require some new strategies."

The main elements of the strategies for the immediate future—until the year 2000—were spelled out in the university's strategic plan made public in October 1993. These are:

Students converse in early May at the base of Mather Sundial in McCosh courtyard.

Remaining roughly the same size. To decrease significantly the size of Princeton's student body, faculty and staff would make it much more difficult to remain a serious center of scholarship, Shapiro explained. But adding substantially to the university's size would make it impossible to maintain academic quality without a massive increase in costs.

Expanding and improving its commitment to teaching. In the face of a nationwide trend among faculty to spend less time in classrooms due to competing pressures, Princeton maintained the quality of its teaching by increasing the size of its faculty over the past 15 years to return the student-faculty ratio to pre-coeducation levels. But further increases are no longer feasible, said Shapiro, as educational costs have outstripped the rate of growth of family income. In his view, Princeton faculty members, who already work extremely hard, will have to adjust their priorities by doing more in the classroom and less of something else, "whether that is attending international meetings, serving on committees in Washington, their own research or service to the community."

Sustaining its capacity for excellence, leadership and new initiatives in scholarship and research. It is likely that in an era of declining levels of sponsored research, especially from the federal government, Princeton will have to devote more of its own resources to research if it is to continue to be a great research university. The aim is to support faculty-initiated scholarship and graduate education in existing disciplines, while having the flexibility to pursue important new fields as the university did in creating the departments of Molecular Biology and Computer Science, the programs in Women's Studies and Afro-American Studies, and dozens of other new courses and special programs.

Maintaining its strong commitment to financial aid for undergraduates and graduate students. To sustain its quality and diversity, the university aims to improve its financial aid for students from low- and middle-income families and to remove the current limit on financial aid to students from other countries, who are not eligible for U. S. government programs. In an age of global markets and global communications, in Shapiro's view, "we are going to have to take much more seriously the role of international students coming to Princeton and the role of our students studying abroad than we have in the last generation."

Improving the quality of campus life. A planning committee on campus life reported, "Princeton is abundantly endowed with private spaces and buildings but...we lack the kinds of common spaces and facilities that effectively claim the allegiance of different groups." To remedy this, a top priority is construction of a new campus center to encourage a stronger sense of community among all parts of a Princeton student body and faculty that have become much more diverse. In the same pursuit, Princeton aims to provide more common spaces, such as classrooms, computer clusters and lounges in student dormitories as well as to upgrade the living quarters in other ways.

If the plans are properly executed and someone comes back in 20 years, Shapiro told me, "They will know it is a different world; they will know there is a different generation here; they will know that it is not precisely the same Princeton they left and understood and knew. But they are going to feel at home.... I believe it will be changed, but within a context that is perfectly recognizable."

North entrance to the Chapel at dusk.

There is a sense, a very real sense, not mystical but plain fact of experience, in which the spirit of truth, of knowledge, of hope, of revelation dwells in a place like this....

WOODROW WILSON

For another perspective, I met over dinner with six undergraduate leaders to hear their views on Princeton's present and their wish lists for its future. Their comments added up to a strong endorsement of the increased diversity and expanded social and lifestyle choices on the campus that have been important developments in the post–World War II Princeton, and a desire to go further in the same directions.

"Being a woman and being a minority, I wasn't sure that I wanted to come to a school like Princeton because of its past," said Amanda Terry '98, who at the time of this discussion was president of the freshman class. "But I think Princeton is opening up now. Princeton is a wonderful place for undergrads and people realize that, and it's attracting people from a diversity of backgrounds. In the future you will be able to say that your mom went here or that you know many minority groups are also thriving here." Other students chimed in on a similar note, approving the increased diversity of the undergraduate body and calling for more. David Calone '96, president of the Undergraduate Student Government (USG) at the time of the discussion, suggested that Princeton's growing domestic diversity should be matched by an increasing number of international students to encourage a greater "world perspective." In the fall of 1994 students from abroad comprised six percent of the entering freshman class.

Women's crew gliding back to the Class of 1887 Boathouse, Lake Carnegie.

How to create a greater sense of unity amid diversity was a common concern. Several students expressed worry at the compartmentalizing effect of the Greek letter fraternities and sororities, which spread to Princeton in the early 1980s and are estimated to engage about 15 percent of the undergraduates at some level of involvement, even though they are not officially recognized by the university and do not have clubhouses or other physical facilities. Their main appeal, the student leaders said, is that they provide single-sex associations and a way for freshmen and sophomores to meet upperclass students in preparation for joining eating clubs.

As for Prospect Avenue, "There are certain aspects of clubs I really don't like, but I can't imagine Princeton without them," said Ian Blasco '95, USG vice president and a club member. "I would definitely like to see a system where they were incorporated a little bit more into the university.... Most seniors are happy in their clubs, no matter which club it is, but have laments that they used to see more people in their [residential] college. It's a mixed bag."

Regarding academic life, "One of Princeton's greatest strengths is the balance it has been able to maintain between being a leading research institution and being committed to undergraduate education, and that balance is going to be increasingly challenged," observed Neysun Mahboubi '97, president of the sophomore class. Mentioning two professors who recently accepted posts at Harvard, he wondered out loud "if Princeton is going to be able to maintain its commitments to its undergraduates, to give undergraduates the benefit of wonderful professors, give them plenty of time to talk with them and know them, and at the same time attract the caliber of professors that make an institution great." Tim Allison '96, USG historian, expressed concern about a deterioration in emphasis on undergraduate education. "I'd like to see more professors teaching their own precepts."

At the same time, the students vigorously endorsed the statement of Marney Sigler '96, a member of the Student

*C*ellist under a maple on Springdale Golf Course in early fall.

Advisory Board for the 250th anniversary, that "approachability is definitely there…. If you are motivated to talk to your professor after class or stick around for five minutes, they're not going to turn you away, even if you're in a lecture class with 300 people." She recalled the extensive help she received from one of her professors when she telephoned him on a Friday afternoon, adding that "it just takes a little initiative." Amanda Terry agreed, recalling that when Toni Morrison won her Nobel prize and her office filled up with reporters, she excused herself to teach her creative writing class. "That's the type of dedication I have felt from a lot of members of the faculty this, my first, year."

Still another assessment came from the eight outside educators who evaluated Princeton in connection with the university's periodic reaccreditation by the Middle States Association of Colleges and Schools. The mid-1994 report of the team, which was headed by Stanford University President Gerhard Casper, declared that "Princeton is in many respects the model of what a private American university should be. Its stewardship of financial and physical resources over its nearly 250-year history and the quality and devotion of its faculty, staff, students and alumni are the envy of many of its peers. In the vast constellation of American higher education, Princeton's accomplishments are formidable."

Princeton is in many respects the model of what a private American university should be.

FROM THE 1994 REPORT OF THE MIDDLE STATES ASSOCIATION OF COLLEGES AND SCHOOLS

The assessment team made several modestly phrased suggestions, including more attention to the implications of changing communications technology, stronger efforts at recruiting African-American students, increased scrutiny of special admissions treatment for outstanding athletes, more emphasis on facilitating undergraduate study abroad, improvements in academic advising and a better connection between the first two years in residential colleges and the upperclass years.

At the same time, the assessment team recognized that Princeton operates under financial constraints that affect all of higher education. It noted that with its large endowment "Princeton, being relatively speaking 'well-off,' may have more of a problem than many other institutions to convince faculty and students that it too must carefully husband its resources."

The visiting educators identified Princeton's "signature" as its outstanding commitment to undergraduate teaching, whether in the form of classes, precepts, seminars, junior papers or senior theses. "In our view, many Princeton faculty teach willingly and teach well," and many already devote "extraordinary hours" to teaching, preparations and grading, the assessment team reported. If even more needs to be done, the team suggested, Princeton might consider revising such faculty-intensive requirements as junior papers and might also enhance the place of teaching in the criteria for faculty advancement.

"Princeton is a university with a strong sense of shared purpose," the assessment team concluded. "What it wants to accomplish is clear and admirable. It understands that the essence of a university is 'the rubbing of mind against mind,' that teaching, learning and research are not separate activities but, in a great university, different aspects of the all-encompassing search to know."

My own view is that the university that John Witherspoon, James McCosh and Woodrow Wilson marked with distinction and that Harold Dodds, Robert Goheen, William Bowen and Harold Shapiro brought into the contemporary era, has been able to adjust to new times while remaining true to its goals as a center of learning and a spur to public service. There has been no revolutionary break with the past, but a successful

*P*roctor tiger, installed at the north entrance to Nassau Hall in 1911.

evolution. Princeton's is a strong culture, bearing the indelible imprint of its history even while marching into the future.

On the day of my graduation in June 1952, Harry Truman was in the White House, Joseph Stalin was in the Kremlin, the United States was at war in Korea, and the Cold War was at a peak of intensity. This was before the coming of birth control pills, aerosol sprays and personal computers, the outlawing of racial segregation in public schools and accommodations, the rise of television to great popularity and impact, the widespread movement toward equality for women, or the orbiting of space satellites that make possible the global market and global means of mass communications. Rarely has change taken place so swiftly and with such powerful consequences.

Princeton has been able to change with the times, it seems to me, on something of its own terms, without compromising its purposes or its standards. That is no small achievement with which to face the future.

Female Siberian tiger in the Faculty Room of Nassau Hall in 1995, for a film commemorating Princeton's 250th anniversary.

Alumni and Reunions

The loyalty and dedication—some might say, fanaticism—of Princeton's alumni are extraordinary.

As of 1995, living undergraduate alumni numbered about 50,000. In any given year, roughly 6,000 to 8,000 do volunteer work of some kind for the university, primarily as class officers, officers of the 150 Princeton clubs or regional associations throughout the United States and in 21 other countries, or as members of schools committees that identify, encourage and interview applicants to Princeton. More than 53 percent, or close to 27,000 alumni, pay class dues. An even larger number, more than 56 percent, contributed to Annual Giving in 1994-95, giving a whopping total of more than $21 million. Providing information and a shared connection to developments and issues on the campus is the *Princeton Alumni Weekly*, which is no longer published weekly but still, at 17 issues per year, is published more frequently than any other alumni magazine in the United States. Graduate school alumni, who number about 17,000, have become increasingly active in recent years, especially through the Association of Princeton Graduate Alumni.

As impressive as they are, mere statistics understate the strength of the ties that bind a large percentage of Princeton alumni. Yes, for the university there is respect, affection, loyalty and pride. But for one's Princeton contemporaries, and especially classmates, these qualities apply even more. For many Princeton graduates, the author included, ties with classmates are among the strongest and most enduring friendships of their lives.

The story is told that Christian Gauss, the legendary early 20th-century professor and dean of the college, was asked at a freshman orientation meeting why there weren't any fraternities at Princeton. Gauss replied that this wasn't exactly true: "You'll find your class is the finest fraternity in America, and you will belong to it for a lifetime." Dan White '65, director of the Alumni Council, who has investigated classmate relationships with greater intensity than most Princetonians, wrote in an essay in his class's 25th reunion book that resilient and long-lasting Princeton ties are more than friendships. "They are what we might not have said they were in the old Princeton, before co-education. They are loving relationships." Whether the personal contact is frequent or infrequent, these are often relationships of such enduring quality that they can be picked up at almost a moment's notice where they were interrupted months, years or even decades before.

The ultimate expression of Princeton camaraderie is reunions, the annual festival that brings 5,000 to 6,000 alumni organized by class and about an equal number of spouses, children and significant others to the campus the weekend before commencement. Some alumni, especially those living near Princeton, attend their class reunions annually, and many more attend the larger reunion celebrations at five-year intervals marking significant anniversaries of their graduation.

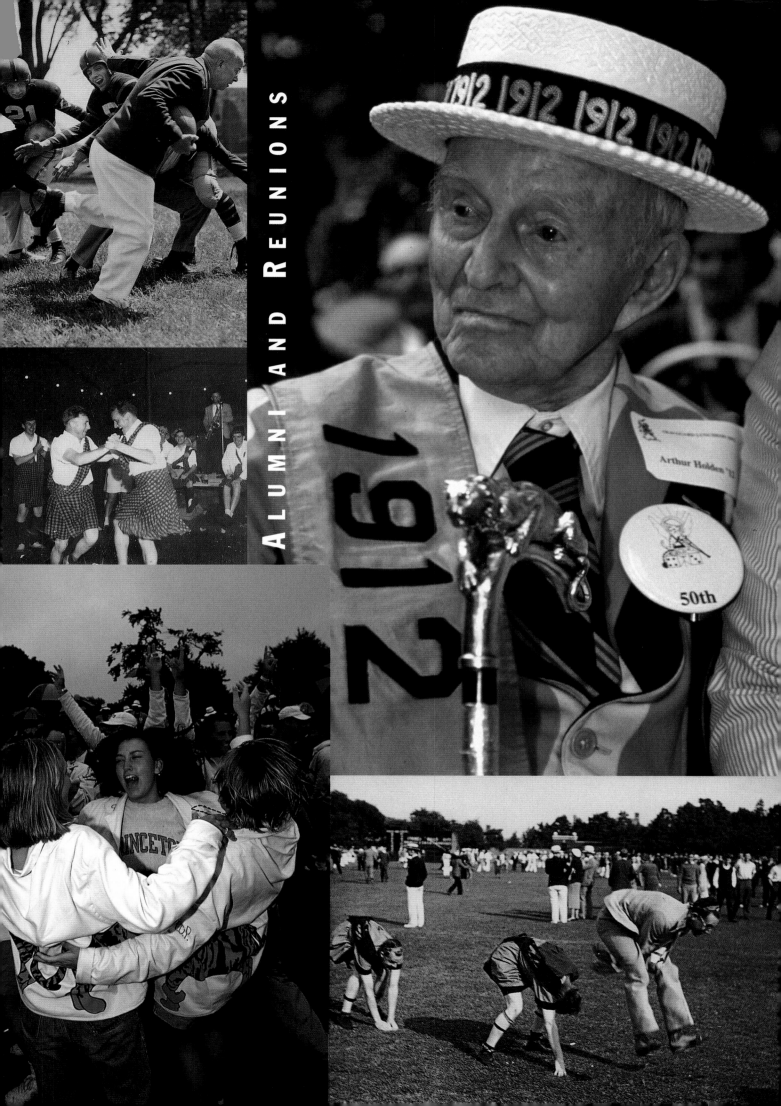

Reunions date back to the early days of the university, when graduates returned at commencement to visit professors and friends. By 1826, when James Madison was named the first president of the newly formed alumni association, the steward of the college was serving a special dinner at commencement to alumni guests. By the turn of the century, reunions had become a major event, sometimes beginning as long as a week before commencement. The P-rade, the annual procession of classes, many in costume and bearing class banners, began in 1906. It has become the dramatic and often emotional high point of reunion weekends. An intellectual high point is the alumni-faculty forum program that was initiated in 1951 by the Class of 1926.

With the arrival of coeducation and greater student diversity and the expansion of the undergraduate student body by about one-third, doubts arose whether the younger classes would experience the same strong bonds as the smaller, more traditional classes that came before. The evidence to date is encouraging. In June 1995 more than 650 of the 1,100 members of the Class of 1990 attended their fifth reunion, and other young classes also have been setting records for participation. Many of the 11,000 women now among Princeton's undergraduate alumni are extremely active; in 1994-95, women served as presidents of 11 of the 15 most recent alumni classes.

ALUMNI AND REUNIONS

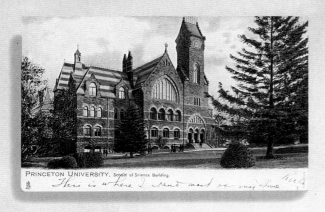

Green School of Science, 1874-1928. (2)

Dickinson Hall, 1870-1920. (3)

Halstead Observatory, 1868-1932. (9)

Old Dinky train station, 1896-1917. (10)

The Vanished Campus

The Princeton campus has evolved by subtraction as well as addition. The eight postcards above depict university buildings that have disappeared over the course of this century. This bird's eye view, published in 1875 during the presidency of James McCosh, anticipated the completion of Witherspoon Hall (1), which was not finished until 1877. Now-vanished buildings include the Green School of Science (2), Dickinson Hall (3), the Old Chapel (4), East College (5), Reunion Hall (6), Bonner-Marquand Gymnasium (7), University Hall (8), the Halstead Observatory (9) and the old train station (10). The original wood and stucco Whig (11) and Clio (12) buildings were replaced by marble structures in 1893. The houses along Nassau Street between University Hall and the Presbyterian church (13) were private residences.

Bonner-Marquand Gymnasium, 1870-1908. (7)

University Hotel (later Hall), 1876-1916. (8)

Art Museum, 1892-1964.

Upper Pyne Hall, 1897-1963. (Lower Pyne, far right, still stands.)

A Princeton Chronology

The College of New Jersey

1696
Town of Princeton settled.

1746
College of New Jersey founded in Elizabeth, New Jersey.

1747
College moves to Newark.

1748
Present charter granted.

1

1753
Nathaniel and Rebeckah FitzRandolph and others deed 10 acres in Princeton to the college.

1756
Nassau Hall and Maclean House completed; College of New Jersey moves from Newark to Princeton.

1768
The Reverend John Witherspoon of Scotland installed as sixth president.

1769
American Whig Society formed.

2

1770
Cliosophic Society formed.

1776
President Witherspoon signs the Declaration of Independence.

1777
In Battle of Princeton, British are driven from Nassau Hall.

1783
Continental Congress meets in Nassau Hall, which serves as the capitol of the United States from June until November.

1804
The college constructs its third building, renamed Stanhope Hall in 1915.

1826
James Madison, Class of 1771 and former President of the United States, becomes the first president of the alumni association.

1836
West College constructed as a dormitory.

1868
James McCosh of Scotland elected 11th president.

4

1876
The *Princetonian* is published for the first time; becomes a daily in 1892.

1878
Prospect becomes president's house.

1879
Earned doctorates awarded for the first time.

3

1883
Triangle Club (originally called Princeton College Dramatic Association) founded.

1888
Princeton University Art Museum founded.

1893
Honor system established.

1894
Alexander Hall constructed.

5

1. Aula Nassovica, March 1760, the earliest known image of Nassau Hall.

2. Rollerbladers whiz past Whig Hall, 1994.

3. Frederic E. Fox '39 (left) and T. Berry Brazelton '40 in Triangle's 1938-39 production, Once Over Lightly.

4. Revolutionary War cannonball.

5. Postcard of Alexander Hall.

6. *Commencement program, 1897.*

7. *Palmer Stadium program, 1916.*

8. *Basketball players Foster Cooper '53 and John McCune '52 in 1951.*

9. *Suzanne Keller, Princeton's first tenured woman faculty member, in 1968.*

10. *A celebrating tiger.*

1896
Name officially changed to Princeton University; sesquicentennial address: "Princeton in the Nation's Service."

6

7

1900
Graduate school established.

1902
Woodrow Wilson, Class of 1879, elected 13th president.

1905
President Wilson establishes system of preceptorials by junior faculty.

1906
Carnegie Lake created by Andrew Carnegie.

1913
Graduate College dedicated.

1914
Palmer Stadium completed.

1919
School of Architecture established.

1921
School of Engineering established.

1928
Princeton University Chapel dedicated.

1930
School of Public and International Affairs established.

1933
Albert Einstein becomes a life member of the Institute for Advanced Study, with an office on the Princeton campus.

1940
Program of Annual Giving established. Undergraduate radio station (then WPRU, now WPRB) founded.

1947
Dillon Gym constructed.

1948
Firestone Library dedicated.

1951
Forrestal campus established on U.S. Route 1; Project Matterhorn research in nuclear fusion begins there. In 1961 its name is changed to the Princeton Plasma Physics Laboratory.

1962
$53 million fundraising campaign concludes. It exceeds its goal and raises $61 million.

1964
Ph.D degree awarded to a woman for the first time.

9

1969
Trustees vote to admit women undergraduates; Jadwin Gym constructed.

1970
Council of the Princeton University Community (CPUC), a deliberative body of faculty, students, staff and alumni, is established.

1971
Third World Center founded.

1982
System of residential colleges established.

1986
A five-year "Campaign for Princeton" concludes after raising $410.5 million.

1996
Princeton celebrates its 250th anniversary.

10

8

Illustration Credits

Annual of Scientific Discovery, 1852: 52 (Henry). *Bric-a-Brac:* 182 (group), 183 (coed week), 191 (cane spree), 202 (Helm), 237 (game) and 243. L.H. Butterfield, *Letters of Benjamin Rush* (Princeton University Press, 1951): 45. *Daily Princetonian:* 198 (banner) and 238 (cartoon by Peter Schweid '73). William K. Evans postcard collection: 58, 75 (chapel), 96, 108, 161, 176 and 266-267 (see also Evans' book, *A Picture Postcard History of Princeton and Princeton University* [Almar Press, 1993]). E.W. Fox: 11 (watercolor). George Bush Presidential Library, Houston, Texas:112 (Baker and Bush). W.J. Lane '25, ed., *A Pictorial History of Princeton* (Princeton University Press, 1947): 83 (Goldie). National Baseball Library and Archives, Cooperstown, N.Y.: 127 (medal). National Portrait Gallery, Smithsonian Institution/Art Resource, N.Y.: 26 (Lee). *New Yorker:* 187 (cover by Charles E. Martin © 1979 New Yorker, Inc. All rights reserved). *Newsweek:* 112 (Nader © 1968 Newsweek, Inc. All rights reserved). Pressens Bild, Stockholm: 231 (Bardeen ©1956; Morrison ©1993 Jan Collsioo). *Princeton Alumni Weekly:* 182 (Meservey). Princeton University, *The Princeton Book* (Riverside Press, 1879): 18 (seal), 49 (Tusculum) and 226 (house). Princeton University, *Princeton Sesquicentennial Celebration* (Charles Scribner's Sons, 1898): 40 and 98. Princeton University Press: 105 (book). W.B. Scott, ed., *Princeton University Expeditions to Patagonia, 1896-99* (J. Pierpont Morgan Fund): 36 (phrygilus) and 37 (Nassauica). *Sports Illustrated:* 193 (Bradley cover © 1964 Sports Illustrated, Inc. All rights reserved). Maria Templeton: 38-39. *Time:* 193 (cover © 1951 Time, Inc. All rights reserved) and 217 (cover © 1939 Time, Inc. All rights reserved). U.S. Army: 190. U.S. Dept. of the Interior: 207 (letter). U.S. Dept. of the Treasury, Bureau of Printing and Engraving: 110. U.S. Geological Survey, EROS Data Center, Sioux Falls, South Dakota: 36 (glacier). U.S. National Aeronautics and Space Administration: 205 (Conrad). University of California, Berkeley: 93 (Farrand by S.C. Sears © Documents Collection, College of Environmental Design, U.C. Berkeley). Ezra Warner, *Generals in Gray* (Louisiana State University Press, 1959): 61 (Archer, Branch).

Photographers

Denise Applewhite: 8-9, 48 (2 of orrery). Marie Bellis: 186 (valedictorian, salutatorian). Ted Bowell: 36 (asteroid). Ron Carter: 245 (students). Nat Clymer: 228 (dance © 1994), 246 (lacrosse © 1994), 261 (bottom © 1994), 262 (bottom left © 1993), 263 (upper right, bottom left © 1993) and 265 (top left © 1994). John Epstein '96: 246 (in cap © 1994). Elliott Erwitt: 144 (© 1955). Matthew Findlay *94: 36 (cafe). Lawrence French: 112 (Shultz), 189 (field hockey, hockey, lacrosse) and 247 (with grandson). Gerhard Joren: 154 (cover © 1994). Daniel Long: 226 (telescope © 1994). Mahlon Lovett: dust jacket (Miller). Fred Maroon: 172 (reunions © 1965). J.T.

Miller '70: 2-3, 14 (coat of arms), 22, 28, 35 (bonfire), 68 (Little, Nassau, Rainwater tigers), 69 (Borglum, Clio tigers), 91, 92 (Thomson), 106 (Institute), 140, 149-151, 162 (Scheide), 170, 210 (locusts), 213 (cover), 214-215, 218-219, 223 (Robertson), 227, 231 (Taylor, Anderson, Fitch), 242 (Wu), 245 (courtyard), 248-252, 254-259, 265 (top right), 268 (Whig), 272 (gargoyles), dust jacket (Oberdorfer), all © 1995. Robert P. Matthews: 15, 33 (mace), 52 (telegraph), 53 (globe), 113 (Kopp), 174-175, 176 (tiger), 192 (Goodfellow), 210 (demonstration), 211 (Dylan, gates), 222 (class), 232-233 and 244 (Frank, Butler staff). John W.H. Simpson '66: 25 (Holder Arch) and 35 (protest).

Princeton University

Alumni Records Office: 129. Athletic Communications: 127 (Berg by O.J. Turner) and 188. Art Museum: 19 (C.O. von Kienbusch, Jr. '06 Memorial Collection) and 126 (bust, John B. Putnam, Jr. '45 Memorial Collection) (both photographed by Bruce White). Chapel: 11 (glass), 12, 46 (glass) and 159 (glass). Communications and Publications: 7, 185 (Pyne) and 269 (Keller). Department of Physics Archives: 117. Department of Geological Sciences Archives: 161 (paleontologists). Development Communications: 242 (Venturi and Forbes). Fine Hall Library: 221 (logic machine). Geophysical Fluid Dynamics Laboratory): 171 (fluid flow by Isaac Held; vortex by Hamilton, Kevin et al.). Gest Oriental Library: 225 (all). Museum of Natural History, Guyot Hall: 37 (pterygotus) and 161 (fossil). Princeton Blairstown Center: 191 (Lynch). Princeton Plasma Physics Laboratory: 167 (aerial) and 169 (tokamak by Dietmar Krause, plasma by Sidney Medley). Princeton Portrait Collection: 13 (Tennent by Jacob Eichholtz, gift of Miss Smith, subject's granddaughter), 16 (Burr, attributed to Gilbert Stuart, gift of William Otis Morse '02 on behalf of Harriet Burr Morse and Marie Burr Curran), 29, 41 (gift of friends, 1922), 42 (Stockton, attributed to John Wollaston, bequest of Mrs. Alexander T. McGill), 43 (Stockton, bequest of Mrs. Alexander T. McGill), 46 (Madison by John Vanderlyn, gift of Dean Mathey '12 and the Bunbury Co., Inc.), 78 (painting), 84, 130 (portrait by Paul Trebilcock, gift of an anonymous alumnus, 1954), 156 (by James E. Fraser), 157 (by Joy Buba, gift of Jarvis Cromwell '18) and 220 (Green by Daniel Huntington, gift of Mrs. John Cleve Green). Items from the Princeton Portrait Collection were photographed by Bruce White. University Libraries, Department of Rare Books and Special Collections, Manuscripts Division: 17, 47 (letter, John Witherspoon Collection, gift of Moses Taylor Pyne, Class of 1877), 51 (book), 53 (Jerome by Thomas Nast, Caroline Newton Papers, estate of Caroline Newton), 64 (envelope, estate of Henry Clay Cammeron, Class of 1847), 121 (dust jacket, F. Scott Fitzgerald Papers, gift of Mrs. Samuel J. Lanahan, courtesy Charles Scribner III '71),126 (Einstein by Alan Richards, gift of the photographer) and 163 (Koran, Garrett Collection of Islamic Mauscripts, gift of Robert Garrett, Class of 1897). Rare Books Division: 10 (Grenville Kane Collection), 20-21, 162 (Blake, Caroline Newton Collection, gift of Caroline Newton; Alexander coin, Numismatics Collection, gift of David Magie; Macrinus coin, Numismatics Collection, gift of Moses Taylor Pyne, Class of 1877) and 183 (squirrels, gift of Edwin N. Benson, Jr., Class of 1899, and Mrs. Benson in memory of Peter Benson '38). Visual Materials Division: 25 (Nassau Hall, gift of A.E. Vondermuhll '01 and alumni), 27 (gift of Junius Spencer Morgan, Class of 1888), 42 (medallion), 47 (decanter, gift of John Witherspoon Woods '32) and 56 (medals). Graphic Arts: cover (estate of Albridge C. Smith III '36), 14 (Belcher by R. Phillips and J. Faber), 18 (stagecoach, gift of Arthur Collins, Jr. '52), 23 (William III, gift of John Douglass Gordon '05), 30 (estate of Albridge C. Smith III '36), 31 (lithograph by F. Childs, gift of Leonard L. Milberg '53; woodcut), 34 (stamps, gift of Dale Roylance), 50 (gift of Alfred A. Woodhull, Class of 1856), 53 ("Awful Explosion of the 'Peace-Maker' on Board the U.S. Steam Frigate Princeton on Wednesday, 28th Feby. 1844" by Nathaniel Currier, gift of six alumni, 1940), 65 (Sinclair Hamilton Collection, gift of Sinclair Hamilton '06), 93 (drawing by W.F. Shellman '41, gift of the artist), 122 (cartoon by David Levine), 139 (Dillon, estate of Albridge C. Smith III '36), 159 (woodcut by Hans A. Mueller, 1950), 177 (woman with pennant), 235 (Holder tower), 239 (by J. Brody Neuenschwander '81, gift of the artist), 240 (watercolor, estate of Albridge C. Smith III '36) and 266-267 ("Princeton College Bird's Eye View, 1875" by C. O. Hudnut, estate of Albridge C. Smith III '36). All items from the Department of Rare Books and Special Collections were photographed by John Blazejewski.

Illustrations were provided by courtesy of the following: 23 (coat of arms, Nassau Club), 44 (Medical Library, Pennsylvania Hospital, Philadelphia), 147 (Ernest Gordon), 155 (Mathey, Mathey College), 164 ("jade," John Wheeler), 168 (Spitzer, Lyman Spitzer *38), 197 (shirt, Jan Kubik '70), 216 (batik, Martin Kreitman), 217 (Drosophila, Nancy Hawkins), 220 (shield, Yannis Kevrekidis), 221 (Harms, Daniel Rubenstein), 224 (perovskite, Nan Yao, Alexandra Navrotsky and Kurt Leinenweber), 228 (portrait, Visual Arts program), 229 (Malkiel, Burton Malkiel *64), 230 (cover and coin, Lady Gladys Lewis), 231 (stamp, Toni Morrison), 240 (exercise room, Mathey College), 241 (watercolor by Richard Lesure '87, Wilson College), 241 (woman, Mathey College) and 242 (cover of *Architectural Record*, Venturi Scott Brown Associates).

All illustrations not otherwise attributed above or in captions are from the University Archives in the Seeley G. Mudd Manuscript Library, Department of Rare Books and Special Collections, Princeton University Libraries. Individual photographers (where known) are Ollie Atkins: 166; Brown Brothers: 153 (Carnegie); Todd Faulkner: 148 (Davis); Bob Glass: 184 (Herman); Landon Jones '66: 204, 206 (both), 207 (Hickel); Melvin McCray:148 (Fields); Ann Meuer: 172 (campus model); Nelson Morris: 142-143 (all); Pach Brothers: 66; Bill Pierce: 197 (happening), 202 (Kaminsky), 203; Wells Raney: 146; Alan Richards: 221 (von Neumann, gift of the Class of 1946); Howard Schrader: 173 (Murrow); George Small '45: 104 (Gauss); Willard Starks: 48 (Ashworth); Orren Jack Turner: 114-115, 116 (flour), 152 (Pyne); Underwood and Underwood: 97; George Warren: 59; and Wayman Williams: 33 (students). Items were photographed by Denise Applewhite and Robert P. Matthews, with assistance from Robert W. Heil.

Acknowledgements

The author gratefully acknowledges assistance from the dozens of members of the Princeton administration, faculty, staff and student body, as well as alumni, who made the research and writing of this book possible. I am particularly grateful for the research assistance of Geoffrey Plank, a graduate student in the department of History, and Melissa Johnson, and for the help of the archivist Ben Primer and assistant archivists Nanci Young and Dan Linke and their staff at the university's Mudd Manuscript Library, which is a treasure trove of Princetoniana.

The most useful and authoritative published sources on the history of Princeton University are Professor Thomas Jefferson Wertenbaker's bicentennial history, *Princeton 1746-1896* (Princeton University Press, 1946) and *A Princeton Companion* by former university secretary Alexander Leitch '24 (Princeton University Press, 1978).

I also found the following works particularly useful:

Books: *The Half-Opened Door*, by Marcia Graham Synnott (Greenwood Press, 1979); *Club Life at Princeton*, by William K. Selden '34 (Princeton Prospect Foundation, 1995); *The Orange & Black in Black & White*, by the *Daily Princetonian* (1992).

Manuscripts: "A Brief Sketch of the Development of the Princeton Plan of Undergraduate Instruction," by Professor Joseph R. Strayer '25, 1953.

Articles: "The Rise of Student Power," by Richard K. Rein '69, *Princeton Alumni Weekly*, May 23, 1972; "Coeducation at Princeton: The struggle of an idea at a university in transition," by Luther Munford '71, *Daily Princetonian*, Oct. 21, 1969; "The Curious History of Physics at Princeton," by John D. Davies '41, *Princeton Alumni Weekly*, Oct. 2, 1973; "Backing into Sponsored Research: Physics and Engineering at Princeton University, 1945-70," by Amy Sue Blix, *History of Higher Education Annual 1993*.

Senior theses: "Student Activism at Princeton University from 1967 to 1970," Francis P. Sharry, Jr. '78; "Princeton, 1920 to 1929, An Historical Study of a Problem in Reputation," by Michael David Robbins '55; "Princeton University Admissions Policy: The Question of Diversity," by Toni Y. McCall '85; "The Princeton Strike of May 1970," by John Merritt McEnany '72; "Science in a 'Time of Crisis,'" by Russell B. Olwell '91; "The Impact of Black Students on Princeton University," by Ronald P. Munger '79; "Trends in Princeton Admissions," by George E. Tomberlin '71.

Term paper: "'Women May Apply'" by Andrea Rolla '97.

The illustrations editor is grateful to many alumni, faculty, students, staff and townspeople, as well as people with no connection to Princeton, for their help and enthusiasm.

In addition to the individuals at Mudd Library mentioned by the author, I also wish to thank Monica Ruscil, who aided my research on scores of occasions.

The Department of Rare Books and Special Collections at Firestone Library is a mother lode of visual riches, and nearly everyone there advanced this project in some way. I want especially to thank Dale Roylance, curator of graphic arts, for his invaluable assistance with both materials and captions. I also want to thank Stephen Ferguson and Don Skemer, curators respectively of rare books and manuscripts, for their creative suggestions and their help.

Others on campus who deserve special thanks are Robert Clark, professor of art and archaeology; Karen Richter of the Art Museum; James McPherson, George Henry Davis '86 Professor of American History; Jacquelyn Savani, associate communications director for news; Patty Gaspari-Bridges, geology librarian; and Robert Matthews, university photographer for more than 30 years.

William K. Evans, author of *A Picture Postcard History of Princeton and Princeton University* (Almar Press, 1993), was exceedingly generous in allowing me free access to his superb postcard collection. Hugh Wynne '39 and A. Glenn Paul '79 were both valuable sources of advice and inspiration, as was Wanda Gunning, past president of the Historical Society of Princeton. Romus Broadway gave me insight into the Princeton experience of African-Americans; Charles Aquilina, a high school history teacher, contributed a scholarly reconstruction of the parsonage where Princeton was born; and Ted Bowell of the Lowell Observatory in Arizona helped me locate the asteroid "Princetonia" and has offered to name a new discovery after Princeton's 250th.

Books that were central sources included: *Princeton Portraits*, by Donald D. Egbert '24 (Princeton University Press, 1947); *The Princeton Book* (The Riverside Press, 1879); *Pictorial History of Princeton*, by Wheaton J. Lane '25 (Princeton University Press, 1947); *Roaring at One Hundred*, by *The Princeton Tiger* (1983); *Princeton Architecture*, by C.M. Greiff, M.W. Gibbons and E.G.C. Menzies (Princeton University Press, 1967); *Vignettes of Princeton University*, by William K. Selden '34 (Princeton University, 1987); and many of the 94 bound volumes of the *Princeton Alumni Weekly*.

Posthumous medals of honor should go to two great Princetonians, Freddie Fox '39 and John W.H. Simpson '66. I hope my work embodies their spirits in some small way.

Don Oberdorfer '52

J. T. Miller '70